D1192869

GIFTS THAT
MAKE A DIFFERENCE

Gifts that Make a Difference

HOW TO BUY HUNDREDS OF GREAT GIFTS SOLD THROUGH NONPROFITS

Ellen Berry
Foxglove Publishing

GIFTS THAT
MAKE A DIFFERENCE

HOW TO BUY HUNDREDS OF GREAT GIFTS
SOLD THROUGH NONPROFITS

Cover and text design: Kay Selke ♦ Cover illustration: Mohammed Masoor
Illustrations: Leslie Shattuck ♦ Typography: The Mazer Corporation

Publisher's Cataloging in Publication
(Prepared by *Quality Books Inc.*)

Berry, Ellen, 1947-
    Gifts that make a difference: how to buy hundreds of great
gifts sold through nonprofits / Ellen Berry.
    p. cm.
    Includes bibliographical references and index.
    ISBN 0-9633126-6-9

    1. Gifts. 2. Corporations, Nonprofit-Marketing. 3. Giftwares.
I. Title. II. Title: How to buy hundreds of great gifts sold
through nonprofits.

GT3050.T4 1992   382.33
                                    QB192-10606

Library of Congress Card #92-71865
ISBN# 0-9633126-6-9 $7.95 Softcover

Foxglove Publishing
P.O. Box 292500
Dayton, Ohio 45429-0500
USA

To John and Jennifer
who have made the
most difference in my life

SELFHELP Crafts of the World.
Soapstone frame ◆ $5.50

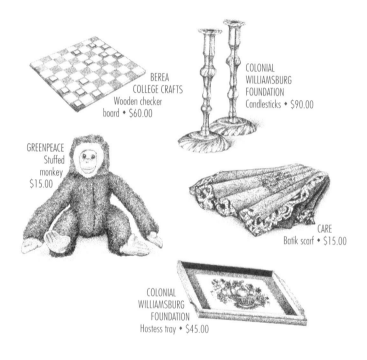

BEREA
COLLEGE CRAFTS
Wooden checker
board ◆ $60.00

COLONIAL
WILLIAMSBURG
FOUNDATION
Candlesticks ◆ $90.00

GREENPEACE
Stuffed
monkey
$15.00

CARE
Batik scarf ◆ $15.00

COLONIAL
WILLIAMSBURG
FOUNDATION
Hostess tray ◆ $45.00

TABLE OF CONTENTS

SECTION ONE

TABLE OF CONTENTS

TABLE OF CONTENTS

TABLE OF CONTENTS

TABLE OF CONTENTS

TABLE OF CONTENTS

SECTION TWO

TABLE OF CONTENTS

SECTION THREE

TABLE OF CONTENTS

CARTOONISTS
ACROSS AMERICA
Theo the Dinosaur
children's book ◆ $9.95

ACKNOWLEDGMENTS

I could not have produced this book without the special people who did all of my other life's work: Joni, thank you for the multitude of tasks that you carried out as my secretary, executive assistant and "wife"; Marlene, thank you for your excellent domestic engineering, dependability and goodness of heart; Lois and Carol, thank you for knowing more about my home than I do and taking care of it; Jane, thank you for your pleasant spirit as you "greened" my home; Tony, thanks for filling so many crazy requests for your sister.

I had wonderful assistance in the construction of this book: Joni, thanks again for all those phone calls, postcards, copies and trips to PKG; Billie, thanks "Sis" for your good-natured help even in the face of catastrophe; Nicole, Teasha and Sterling, thank you for all your copying and miscellaneous helps; Lisa, thank you for your creative help in the beginning; Kay, thank you for being the most patient and competent designer/artist that I could have hoped for; Skip, thanks little brother for the eleventh hour proofreading.

And YPO Famous Forum C has been my very own fan club! Thank you Barbara, Gill, Jane D., Jane S., Jody, Linda, Judy V., Kerry, Loes, Marty and Vicky.

This book began as a chapter in another book. I was compiling a book to be called *Gifts and Good Deeds*. It would be full of unique and personal gift ideas that I had collected in my travels and reading. I began to find gifts that were sold by nonprofits and thought I would include a chapter on these in *Gifts and Good Deeds*. I was surprised to find that there were enough of these nonprofit gifts to fill a book.

This kind of giving was not entirely foreign to me. I had bought Christmas cards from the American Cancer Society. And I had also adopted a wallaby from the Los Angeles Zoo for my godson. Both times I enjoyed knowing that I was helping a good cause. Still I did not think about using the nonprofits as gift shops. I had no idea there was so much available!

When I decided to write *Gifts that Make a Difference*, I confess I had no altruistic motives. I simply thought it was a good idea and that I could accomplish the writing of the book. The responses from the organizations included in the book were overwhelming! "God bless you. We are so thankful for this exposure." "What a great idea! Thanks for including us." "We need this publicity to raise more money for our programs. Thanks for including us."

I have included all of the organizations I could locate that met the criteria by the time my deadline for typeset arrived. The criteria were simply that the organization was not-for-profit and that it had something tangible to sell as part of its fund raising program. The Adopt-A programs have been included because recipients do get the tangible items of a certificate, photo, newsletter, etc. I have not discriminated for or against any cause in the selection of organizations included in this book. I included an organization because it met the two criteria and literature was available to me to confirm this.

It is a satisfying feeling for me to know that my book can be a unique resource of gifts for the reader AND help so many needy and worthwhile causes. You can enjoy the same satisfaction by buying from the nonprofits.

I have tried to make this resource user-friendly.
The following are a few suggestions to help you find
just the perfect gift:

- **If you have an area of interest that you like to support**, look in Section Two to select that category. Choose from among the organizations listed and read the profiles in Section One to see who has an appropriate gift for your needs.

- **If the person you want to give to has a special interest**, find that category in Section Two. Then read the profiles in Section One to choose an organization that has a suitable gift.

- **If you have a type of gift in mind**, find that category in Section Three, and check the organizations' profiles in Section One to find the right gift.

- Unless you are in a particular hurry, it is always best to **call or write for a brochure or catalog** rather than to order an item sight unseen over the telephone. You will then be able to see pictures and prices and ordering information.

- You may want to **send a number of postcards** to selected organizations requesting information on merchandise available. You will be pleasantly surprised to see how many great gifts you can buy especially from the nonprofits who have catalogs. The profiles in Section One indicate whether a catalog is available.

- The extensive **index** can be helpful finding specific items, i.e. linens, dolls, address books, watches.

- **Organizations with large catalogs** (Smithsonian, World Wildlife Fund) have so many items that only the categories of items could be listed. So if the Smithsonian profile does not list dolls but does list toys, it is possible that the Smithsonian does have dolls.

If you would like more information about an organization:

- Ask for reports from the **National Charities Information Bureau** (19 Union Square W., 6th Floor, New York, NY 10003; 212-929-6300). Send an SASE for the "Wise Giving Guide" and up to three reports per request.

- Request information on a particular organization from the **Philanthropic Advisory Service** (PAS) of the Council of Better Business Bureaus (4200 Wilson Blvd., Suite 800, Arlington, VA 22203; 703-276-0100). Send an SASE for "Tips on Charitable Giving" and up to three reports per request.

- Your local **Better Business Bureau** will help you with information on local charitable agencies.

If you would like to buy from local charities not listed in this book:

- Find them in the **yellow pages** under: associations, charitable organizations, foundations, health agencies, health services, human services organizations, social service organizations, youth organizations. The yellow pages index will give you additional headings.

- **Local art institutes, museums and zoos** have gift shops that you may buy from and help support the organization at the same time.

WHAT TO GET FOR EACH PERSON ON YOUR GIFT LIST

Christmas and Birthdays:

Children: Adopt a whale, a wolf, a manatee, a moutain lion, a sea lion, a zoo animal, a farm animal or an injured bird. The child will receive an adoption certificate and other information on his animal. Children love connections to animals and will get an education in the species you adopt for him. I think this is an especially fun gift for godparents and grandparents to give. You can enjoy asking "Have you heard any news lately about your whale?" And the child will enjoy showing you what he has received. Toys and books are also welcome gifts.

Teenagers: Environmental or wildlife T-shirts and other articles of clothing, adopt-an-acre programs, tree planting programs, globes, jewelry, books, calendars, posters, duffel bags.

Adults: Almost anything listed can be a suitable gift for an adult. If you don't know the recipient well, you may consider stationery, calendars, books, gift baskets or desk accessories.

Wedding and Anniversaries: There are many appropriate gifts to select from in the housewares and art categories. A novel gift for an anniversary might be tree plantings in the number of years of the marriage.

Newborns: Tree plantings or adoptions of acreage in rain forests say to the child and his parents that you have hope for his future on this planet. The framed certificate will be an interesting addition to the nursery.

Housewarmings: Trees to plant at home, housewares, art and art objects, gift baskets, gourmet foods, wind chimes.

Father's Day: Pocket knives, mugs, duffel bags, magazine subscriptions, books, belt buckles, hats, jackets, polo shirts, tie tacks, wallets, umbrellas, pens.

Mother's Day: Stationery, figurines, cookbooks, aprons, scarves, stitchery kits, nesting boxes, pewter, jewelry, totes, music boxes, gardening supplies, trays.

Business (for employees or clients): Bronzes, sculptures, prints, original art, paperweights, pens, books, bookends, handcrafts from around the world, tree ornaments, pewter, gift baskets, music boxes, globes. There is added public relations value to a business gift accompanied by a gift card indicating that the item's sale helps support an organization making the world a better place.

DON'T FORGET YOURSELF! You deserve the satisfaction of knowing the merchandise you buy for yourself or your home is making the world a better place too. Also remember to buy the accessories to your gift-giving from the nonprofits: giftwrap, Christmas cards, greeting cards, notecards.

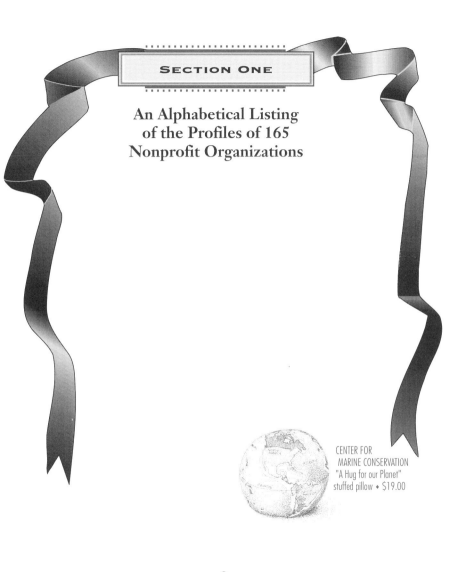

An Alphabetical Listing of the Profiles of 165 Nonprofit Organizations

CENTER FOR
MARINE CONSERVATION
"A Hug for our Planet"
stuffed pillow ◆ $19.00

ACTION ON SMOKING & HEALTH (ASH)

⊸ PURPOSE ⊷
Reduce the deadly toll of smoking through education
and protect the rights of nonsmokers through legal action

⊸ ACTIVITIES ⊷
Education, legal action, and tracking state legislation
regarding smoking; petitioning OSHA to establish smoke-free
workplaces; elimination of smoking on most public transportation;
supporting claims filed for workman's compensation
when smoking is an issue; supporting parents in custody
disputes that involve smoking which threatens a child's health, etc.

⊸ GIFTS ⊷
Paperweights, mugs, tie tacks, pins, key tags

*"Protecting the rights of the nonsmoking majority
because smoking hurts everyone it touches"*

Action on Smoking and Health (ASH)
2013 H Street N.W.
Washington, DC 20006
(202) 659-4310

ADOPT-A-COW

⟜ PURPOSE ⟜
Cow protection

⟜ ACTIVITIES ⟜
A living example of cow protection providing
a cruelty-free life avoiding slaughterhouses; education

⟜ GIFTS ⟜
Adopt-A-Cow: adoption certificate, photo of your cow
or ox, newsletter, updates, starting at $30/month;
T-shirts, caps, sweatshirts, vegetarian cookbooks

*"The most revolutionary cow protection
program in the world"*

Adopt-A-Cow
Gita-nagari Village
R.D. 1, Box 839
Port Royal, PA 17082
(717) 527-4101

AFRICAN WILDLIFE FOUNDATION

⊷ PURPOSE ⊶
Protect the wildlife of Africa and their habitats

⊷ ACTIVITIES ⊶
Conservation education and training;
protected area management;
endangered species protection

⊷ GIFTS ⊶
Books, posters, jewelry

"Only elephants should wear ivory."

African Wildlife Foundation
1717 Massachusetts Avenue, N.W.
Washington, D.C. 20036
(202) 265-8393

THE ALASKA WILDLIFE ALLIANCE

⊸ PURPOSE ⊶
Protect Alaska's wildlife

⊸ ACTIVITIES ⊶
Actions to reform wolf/predator management policy,
reduce illegal hunting and trapping, wildlife advocacy,
reduce disturbance and harrassment of endangered
humpback whales in Glacier Bay National Park

⊸ GIFTS ⊶
Books, calendars, postcards,
pins, T-shirts, sweatshirts, prints

"Help Alaska's Wildlife."

The Alaska Wildlife Alliance
P.O. Box 202022
Anchorage, AK 99520-2022
(907) 277-0897

⊸ PURPOSE ⊱

Marine wildlife research,
education and conservation

⊸ ACTIVITIES ⊱

Field research stations, library of photo-identified
whale information, whale information catalogs

⊸ GIFTS ⊱

Adopt A Finback Whale: adoption certificate, color
photo, a history of your whale and a record of its sightings,
fact sheets, newsletter, $30; T-shirts, mugs, videos,
postcards, posters, books

"The second largest mammal ever to inhabit the earth"

Allied Whale
College of the Atlantic
105 Eden Street
Bar Harbor, ME 04609
(207) 288-5644

ALZHEIMER'S DISEASE RESEARCH

⊸ PURPOSE ⊱
Research of age-related and degenerative diseases

⊸ ACTIVITIES ⊱
This program's parent organization,
American Health Assistance Foundation, educates the public
about Alzheimer's and provides financial assistance
to patients and their caregivers.

⊸ GIFTS ⊱
All-occasion cards

"Better health through research"

Alzheimer's Disease Research
15825 Shady Grove Road,
Suite 140
Rockville, Maryland 20850
(800) 227-7998

⊸ PURPOSE ⊷

Control and eliminate cancer

⊸ ACTIVITIES ⊷

Research, service to
cancer patients, education

⊸ GIFTS ⊷

Holiday greeting cards, ACS cookbook

"Know cancer's warning signals!"

American Cancer Society
Washington Division, Inc.
2120 First Avenue N.
P.O. Box 19140
Seattle, WA 98109-1140
(800) 729-1151

⊸ PURPOSE ⊱
Preserve and protect dolphins and whales

⊸ ACTIVITIES ⊱
Education, research, conservation

⊸ GIFTS ⊱
Books, audios, videos, calendars, posters,
shirts, jewelry, greeting cards, postcards, notecards,
Christmas ornaments

"They're not saved yet."

American Cetacean Society
P.O.Box 2639
San Pedro, CA 90731-0943
(310) 548-6279

AMERICAN DIABETES ASSOCIATION

⊷ PURPOSE ⊶
Discover a preventive
and a cure for diabetes

⊷ ACTIVITIES ⊶
Research

⊷ GIFTS ⊶
Holiday greeting cards, tree ornaments,
stuffed toys, calendars, candles, totes

"Together we can help find a cure."

American Diabetes Association
Holiday Program
680 Mendelssohn Avenue
Golden Valley, MN 55427
(612) 541-1333

AMERICAN FORESTRY ASSOCIATION

⊸ PURPOSE ⊱

Promote tree and forest conservation; encourage
people to plant and care for trees via Global Releaf, the national
and international education and action campaign of AFA

⊸ ACTIVITIES ⊱

Community tree planting and care projects; tropical
forest education program for middle schools; a 900# to call
to have a tree planted in your name and information
sent for a $5 charge to your phone bill

⊸ GIFTS ⊱

Tree plantings (several unique programs): certificate,
starting at $10; a ready-to-plant tree from Walden Woods
seeds, books, T-shirts, caps, mugs, totes, notecards

"The oldest citizens' conservation group"

American Forestry Association
P.O. Box 2000
Washington, DC 20013
(800) 677- 0727 ◆ (202) 667-3300

⤙ PURPOSE ⤚
Alleviate suffering; work for
justice, reconciliation and peace

⤙ ACTIVITIES ⤚
Relief and development projects;
advocacy for human rights and economic
justice; promote peace

⤙ GIFTS ⤚
Notecards, postcards, calendars

"Social justice, humanitarian service and peace"

American Friends Service Committee
1501 Cherry Street, Finance Dept.
Philadelphia, PA 19102
(800) 342-5796

⊰ PURPOSE ⊱
Safeguard the welfare of America's horses

⊰ ACTIVITIES ⊱
Education, legislation, state volunteer program,
seminars, special projects and events

⊰ GIFTS ⊱
T-shirts, sweatshirts, mugs, caps,
books, art, Christmas cards

"For the love of horses..."

American Horse Protection Association, Inc.
1000 29th Street, N.W., Suite T-100
Washington, DC 20077
(202) 965-0500

THE AMERICAN HORTICULTURAL SOCIETY

ⵜ PURPOSE ⵜ
Serve the needs of the American
gardener; promote excellence in horticulture

ⵜ ACTIVITIES ⵜ
Publications, educational programs, travel tours,
seed program, special events, River Farm Garden Park,
exhibitions, National Home Composting Park

ⵜ GIFTS ⵜ
Books, gardening supplies

"Serving American Gardeners since 1922"

The American Horticultural Society
7931 East Boulevard Drive
Alexandria, VA 22308
(800) 777-7931 ♦ (703) 768-5700

AMERICAN LIBRARY ASSOCIATION

⊸ PURPOSE ⊷
Promote reading and using libraries

⊸ ACTIVITIES ⊷
Promotional materials to motivate children
and others to read; celebrity spokespeople

⊸ GIFTS ⊷
Catalog: posters, T-shirts, bookmarks, sports bottles,
stuffed toys, calendars, notecards, postcards,
puppets, totes, neckties, scarves, jewelry

"Read. Succeed."

American Library Association
ALA Graphics
50 E. Huron Street
Chicago, IL 60611
(800) 545-2433, press 8

AMERICAN MINOR BREEDS CONSERVANCY

◄ PURPOSE ►

Conserve rare livestock breeds

◄ ACTIVITIES ►

Provides technical support to breeders
and breed associations, operation of a semen bank,
clearinghouse, education

◄ GIFTS ►

Books, posters, videos,
T-shirts, totes, postcards, notecards

"Saving rare farm animals for the future"

American Minor Breeds Conservancy
P.O. Box 477
Pittsboro, NC 27312
(919) 542-5704

⊷ PURPOSE ⊶
Protection and preservation of America's wild equine

⊷ ACTIVITIES ⊶
Rescue/Rehab/Relocation Service, adoptions,
Abuse/Neglect Hotline, educational programs, shows, clinics,
playdays, referral services, museum, library, registry

⊷ GIFTS ⊶
Books, calendars, T-shirts, sweatshirts, caps,
jewelry, videos, limited edition prints

*"Symbols of the historic and pioneer
spirit of the West"*

American Mustang & Burro Association
P.O. Box 7
Benton City, WA 99320
(509) 588-6336

⊸ PURPOSE ⊸
Restore and preserve America's oceans

⊸ ACTIVITIES ⊸
Education, advocacy, legislation,
Coastal Cleanup Days

⊸ GIFTS ⊸
T-shirts

"Help us turn the tide."

American Oceans Campaign
725 Arizona Avenue, Suite 102
Santa Monica, CA 90401
(213) 576-6162

⊸ PURPOSE ⊱

Preserve and restore America's river
systems and foster a river stewardship ethic

⊸ ACTIVITIES ⊱

Protects rivers in every state; saves
threatened fish and wildlife; defends clean water,
recreation and scenic beauty

⊸ GIFTS ⊱

T-shirts, posters, books, calendars

"Rivers—The nation's circulatory system"

American Rivers
Gift Department, Suite 400
801 Pennsylvania Avenue SE
Washington, DC 20003
(202) 547-6900

⊷ PURPOSE ⊶
The alleviation of fear, pain,
and suffering in the animal world

⊷ ACTIVITIES ⊶
Pet adoptions, animal shelter, Bergh Animal Hospital,
humane education, companion animal services, humane
law enforcement, legal/legislative activities, Animalport

⊷ GIFTS ⊶
Notecards, books, T-shirts,
caps, aprons, mugs, videos, posters

"America's first humane society"

American Society for the Prevention of
Cruelty to Animals (ASPCA)
424 E. 92nd Street
New York, NY 10128
(212) 876-7700

ANIMAL AMBASSADORS INTERNATIONAL

⊷ PURPOSE ⊶
Develop a deeper understanding of
animals and ourselves

⊷ ACTIVITIES ⊶
Sponsor educational programs through school projects;
zoo programs; wildlife rescue and rehabilitation

⊷ GIFTS ⊶
Books, audios

"Celebrating the magic of animals in our lives"

Animal Ambassadors International
P.O.Box 3793
Pojoaque Station
Santa Fe, NM 87501-0793
(505) 455-2945

⊷ Purpose ⊶

Protect and maintain the Appalachian Trail
and adjacent publicly-owned acreage

⊷ Activities ⊶

Acquires threatened lands nearby, briefs Congress
on needs and problems, coordinates volunteer work,
sponsors maintenance crews, Trail policy
development, publications, visitors' center, archives

⊷ Gifts ⊶

Books, calendars, posters, videos, polo shirts,
T-shirts, caps, bandanas, mugs, hip packs

"2,143 miles from Maine to Georgia"

Appalachian Trail Conference
P.O. Box 807, Dept SD
Harpers Ferry, WV 25425
(304) 535-6331

ART INSTITUTE OF CHICAGO

⊸ PURPOSE ⊱
Build and operate museums, schools,
libraries of art, and theatres

⊸ ACTIVITIES ⊱
Exhibit permanent collections of art
and present temporary exhibitions; education

⊸ GIFTS ⊱
Catalog: calendars, stationery, jewelry, scarves,
framed prints, greeting cards, T-shirts, puzzles, giftwrap,
pens, books, toys, sweatshirts, mugs, totes,
umbrellas, home decor, posters

"Visit the Museum Shops in Chicago."

Art Institute of Chicago
125 Armstrong Road
Des Plaines, IL 60018
(800) 621-9337

ASTRONOMICAL SOCIETY OF THE PACIFIC

⊸ PURPOSE ⊢
Science education

⊸ ACTIVITIES ⊢
Nontechnical, authoritative
publications and programs about the universe

⊸ GIFTS ⊢
Catalog: books, slide sets, videos, audios,
computer software, observing aids, posters, postcards,
jewelry, Christmas ornaments, coloring books,
diaries, watches, etc.

*"A bridge between astronomers and
the public since 1889"*

Astronomical Society of the Pacific
390 Ashton Avenue
San Francisco, CA 94112
(415) 337-2624

BACK TO NATURE WILDLIFE

⏤ Purpose ⏤
Refuge for orphaned, injured
and permanently impaired wildlife

⏤ Activities ⏤
Rescue, rehabilitate and release wild animals;
provide a home for the permanently injured, unreleaseable
wild animals; environmental wildlife education

⏤ Gifts ⏤
Adopt-A-Wild-One: adoption certificate,
color photo and the animal's special story, starting at $20

"Your support helps us save and feed the critters."

Back to Nature Wildlife, Inc.
351 East Fourth Street
Chuluota, FL 32766
(407) 366-1394

⊸ PURPOSE ⊱

Discover and foster worldwide efforts to
balance population growth with natural resources

⊸ ACTIVITIES ⊱

Financially supports research activities, exhibits,
publications, conferences, lectures and nature tours that
educate the public on the threat that overpopulation
poses to the world's natural resources

⊸ GIFTS ⊱

Tree plantings (endangered tropical trees):
personalized certificate, $5

"Agriculture production through tropical reforestation"

The Basic Foundation
P.O. Box 47012
St. Petersburg, FL 33743
(813) 526-9562

⊸ PURPOSE ⊸
Conservation of bats and their habitats worldwide

⊸ ACTIVITIES ⊸
Through education, raise awareness of the importance
of bats and the ecosystems that depend on them;
protect critical bat habitats through conservation partnerships
around the world; conduct conservation-related bat research

⊸ GIFTS ⊸
Catalog: posters, bronzes, etchings, books, calendars,
notecards, Christmas cards, clothing, jewelry, banks, suncatchers,
windsocks, wind chimes, fanny packs, lunch bags, coasters,
ornaments, bat houses, bat detectors, slides

*"These gentle friends and essential allies carry the
seeds that make the rain forests grow and the deserts bloom."*

Bat Conservation International, Inc. (BCI)
P. O. Box 162603
Austin, TX 78716-2603
(512) 327-9721

BEREA COLLEGE CRAFTS

⊸ Purpose ⊱
Provide tuition-free education to
all students enrolled at Berea College

⊸ Activities ⊱
Students are employed in one of five craft areas:
Broomcraft, Ceramics, Weaving, Woodcraft, Wrought Iron

⊸ Gifts ⊱
Catalog: games, cutting boards, tableware,
books, baskets, candlesticks, mohair stoles, blankets, porcelain
tea sets, fireplace accessories, brooms, furniture

"Students and master craftspeople work side-by-side."

Berea College Crafts
CPO 2347
Berea, KY 40404
(800) 347-3892

BETTER HOMES FOUNDATION

⊷ PURPOSE ⊶

Help homeless families get back on their feet
and back in the mainstream of America

⊷ ACTIVITIES ⊶

Health care, job training, drug and alcohol
abuse programs, early education for children

⊷ GIFTS ⊶

Catalog: holiday ornaments, notecards, toys,
puzzles, blankets, enamelware, nightshirts, wreaths

"Help for homeless families"

Better Homes Foundation
P.O. Box 9236
Des Moines, IA
50306-9236

BETTY CLOONEY FOUNDATION FOR PERSONS WITH BRAIN INJURY

⌐ PURPOSE ¬

Develop affordable, community-based
vocational, recreational and residential services for
persons who survive brain injury

⌐ ACTIVITIES ¬

Baskets and backpacks are assembled at the
Betty Clooney Center to help members gain experience and
skills in order to return to the community workplace.

⌐ GIFTS ¬

Catalog: survival backpacks; gourmet
food and gift baskets, including custom orders

*"Founded by Rosemary Clooney after the death
of her sister and injury to her cousin from brain injury"*

Betty Clooney Foundation for Persons With Brain Injury
2933 Long Beach Boulevard
Long Beach, CA 90806
(800) 93-GIFT-1, catalog
(310) 426-2881 ♦ (310) 426-0181

BRADDOCK'S FIELD
HISTORICAL SOCIETY

⊰ PURPOSE ⊱
Preserve the rich history of
the Braddock area

⊰ ACTIVITIES ⊱
Braddock Carnegie Library restoration

⊰ GIFTS ⊱
Notecards, mugs,
T-shirts, sweatshirts

"America's oldest Carnegie Library"

Braddock's Field Historical Society
419 Library Street
Braddock, PA 15104
(412) 351-5356

**THE BROOKS
BIRD CLUB**

⊸ PURPOSE ⊱
Promote the study and enjoyment
of birds and other elements of the
natural world

⊸ ACTIVITIES ⊱
Bird population studies,
land acquisition, bird banding,
educational projects

⊸ GIFTS ⊱
Books

"The backyard birdwatcher"

The Brooks Bird Club, Inc.
707 Warwood Avenue
Wheeling, WV 26003

**CAMP FIRE
BOYS AND GIRLS**

⊸ PURPOSE ⊶
Provide opportunities for youth to function
effectively as caring, self-directed individuals; improve
conditions in society which affect youth

⊸ ACTIVITIES ⊶
Camping programs, clubs, self-reliance courses;
youth-run food programs; prevention of crime, drug abuse, teen
suicide, teen pregnancy; school-age child care; youth leadership

⊸ GIFTS ⊶
Catalog: clothing,
club supplies, watches, pens

"For youth to realize their potential"

Camp Fire Boys and Girls
4601 Madison Avenue
Kansas City, MO 64112
(816) 756-1950

CANADIAN PHYSICIANS FOR AID AND RELIEF

⌐ PURPOSE ⌐
Help people in the Third World improve
their lives in harmony with their environment

⌐ ACTIVITIES ⌐
Reforestation programs; improvement of
health care systems; ensure the productive capacity of
the soil and an adequate supply of water

⌐ GIFTS ⌐
Plant A Tree in Africa: color 9" x 23" poster with the
receiver's name and the number of trees sponsored inscribed on
the poster, starting at 100 trees for $25; T-shirts, sweatshirts

"Give a gift that will grow."

Canadian Physicians for Aid and Relief
64 Charles Street East
Toronto, Ontario Canada M4Y 1T1
(416) 961-6786

CARE

⊸ PURPOSE ⊷
Help the developing world's poor in their
efforts to achieve social and economic well-being

⊸ ACTIVITIES ⊷
Health and nutrition programs for mothers
and children; agriculture and reforestation programs;
small-business development; food supplements;
emergency aid to disaster victims

⊸ GIFTS ⊷
Catalog of handmade crafts from around the world:
jewelry, toys, clothing, tableware, home accessories

"CARE helps people help themselves."

CARE
CARE Package Catalog
P.O. Box 684
Holmes, PA 19043-9878
(800) 345-8112

CARIBBEAN CONSERVATION CORP

⊸ PURPOSE ⊱
Conservation of sea turtles and coastal habitats
throughout the Caribbean and the Atlantic

⊸ ACTIVITIES ⊱
Habitat protection, education,
research, conservation, training

⊸ GIFTS ⊱
Adopt-A-Turtle: personal letter,
adoption certificate, turtle fact sheet, a year's
subscription to the newsletter, poster, $20

"No deposit...no return."

Caribbean Conservation Corporation
P.O. Box 2866
Gainesville, FL 32602
(800) 678-7853 ♦ (904) 373-6441

CARTOONISTS ACROSS AMERICA

⊶ PURPOSE ⊷
Promote reading and recycling
with humor in cartoons

⊶ ACTIVITIES ⊷
Gallery, touring, developing materials
promoting reading and recycling, cartoon contest
promoting literacy and education

⊶ GIFTS ⊷
Books, cassette tapes,
T-shirts, mugs

"Read. Avoid extinction."

Cartoonists Across America
P.O. Box 670
Lompoc, CA 93438-0670
(805) 735-5134

THE CENTER FOR ENVIRONMENTAL STUDY

⊸ PURPOSE ⊸
Preserve and enhance the quality of
the global environment through education,
communication and research

⊸ ACTIVITIES ⊸
Tropical forest land acquisition/protection,
reforestation, education, research

⊸ GIFTS ⊸
Adopt An Acre of Tropical Forest:
certificate, $25; trees and seeds to plant,
T-shirts, totes

"Tree Amigos"

The Center for Environmental Study
143 Bostwick NE
Grand Rapids, MI 49503
(616) 771-3935

CENTER FOR MARINE CONSERVATION

⌐ PURPOSE ⌐

Protect endangered marine species; conserve
special marine habitats; prevent marine pollution;
manage fisheries for conservation

⌐ ACTIVITIES ⌐

Policy oriented research, public awareness and
education, support domestic and international conservation
programs, involve citizens in public policy decisions

⌐ GIFTS ⌐

Catalog: marine-themed clothing, accessories,
jewelry, toys, books, audio/video cassettes, sculptures, framed
art, posters, housewares, glassware and crockery

"Dedicated to worldwide protection of marine wildlife and their habitats"

Center for Marine Conservation
1725 DeSales Street, N.W.
Washington, DC 20036
(800) 227-1929, catalog ♦ (202) 429-5609

CENTER FOR REPRODUCTION OF ENDANGERED SPECIES

━ PURPOSE ━
Improve the health, well-being and breeding
potential of rare and endangered species

━ ACTIVITIES ━
Research

━ GIFTS ━
Adopt-An-Animal: adoption certificate, newsletter, $50;
higher donation amounts include free passes to
the San Diego zoo, color photos, and special events

"Send a gift they'll be wild about."

Center for Reproduction of
Endangered Species (CRES)
Zoological Society of San Diego
P.O. Box 271
San Diego, CA 92112
(619) 231-1515

CHICAGO FUND RAISING COMMITTEE TO BENEFIT PEDIATRIC AIDS

⊰ PURPOSE ⊱

Raise awareness and money for
children with AIDS

⊰ ACTIVITIES ⊱

Fund research; support a model program in
Los Angeles for dealing with pediatric AIDS in the
community; emergency assistance; education

⊰ GIFTS ⊱

T-shirts and sweatshirts designed by
Zack, a child who died after contracting AIDS
from a transfusion; tapes and CD's

"Hope for children with AIDS"

Chicago Fund Raising Committee to Benefit Pediatric AIDS
Zack's Shirt Fund
P.O. Box 181
Glencoe, IL 60022
(708) 835-1689

CHICAGO ZOOLOGICAL SOCIETY

⟜ PURPOSE ⟞
Preservation of threatened species

⟜ ACTIVITIES ⟞
Zoological park, research,
captive breeding programs

⟜ GIFTS ⟞
Adopt-An-Animal: adoption certificate,
newsletter, an exclusive evening for parents at the zoo, $25

"Want a critter you can call your very own?"

Chicago Zoological Society
Brookfield Zoo Parents Program
Brookfield, IL 60513
(708) 485-0263

⊸ PURPOSE ⊸
Support multidisciplinary treatment for
children with cancer and related blood diseases

⊸ ACTIVITIES ⊸
Support for medical treatment, social services
and financial assistance to children who are patients at
the H. Lee Moffitt Cancer Center

⊸ GIFTS ⊸
Greeting cards designed by children

"A research program on the cutting edge"

Children's Cancer Center, Inc.
at H. Lee Moffitt Cancer Center & Research Institute
12901 Bruce B. Downs Blvd., Box 37
Tampa, FL 33612
(813) 972-4673, ext. 2128

⤙ PURPOSE ⤚

Help children thrive and attain their full potential by
providing support and by strengthening their families

⤙ ACTIVITIES ⤚

Statewide services in the areas of residential care, foster
care, family support, counseling, adoption support, volunteer
support, day treatment and advocacy

⤙ GIFTS ⤚

Gift boxes of Red Delicious and Granny Smith apples or Bosc
and Anjou pears (6, 12 or 24), with or without cheddar/monterey jack
cheese; giant caramel and chocolate covered apples;
gourmet Walla Walla sweet onions

*"Give the gift that gives twice, once to your recipient
and again to the children who benefit from your purchase."*

Children's Home Society of Washington
P.O. Box 15190
Seattle, WA 98115-0190
(800) 456-3338

CHURCH WORLD SERVICE/CROP

⊣ PURPOSE ⊢
Help poor families move towards self-sufficiency;
respond to emergencies; provide assistance to refugees

⊣ ACTIVITIES ⊢
Domestic: CROP Walks for the Hungry;
educational events; blanket offerings
Overseas (in over 70 countries): preventive health care;
digging wells; food, medicine and clothing
to refugees; improvement in food production

⊣ GIFTS ⊢
Posters, notecards, calendars,
greeting cards

"Help CROP stop hunger."

Church World Service/CROP
P.O. Box 968
Elkhart, IN 46515-0968
(219) 264-3102

⊸ PURPOSE ⊱
Wildlife preservation

⊸ ACTIVITIES ⊱
Zoo and botanical garden,
education, conservation, research, recreation

⊸ GIFTS ⊱
ADOPT-An-Animal program: adoption certificate, color
photo of "adopted"animal, window decal, invitation to "Parents"
Night event, donor recognition on ADOPT board, $30

"Become a partner in conservation."

Cincinnati Zoo and Botanical Garden
3400 Vine Street
Cincinnati, OH 45220
(513) 559-7724

⤙ PURPOSE ⤚

Promote independence and self-sufficiency for
children and their families living in coffee-growing communities

⤙ ACTIVITIES ⤚

Raising funds to support projects that improve
health and sanitation; teach proper nutrition and child care;
promote education and community development;
promote environmentally sound agriculture

⤙ GIFTS ⤚

T-shirts, sweatshirts, caps, totes, mugs

*"Improve the quality of life for children and
families from coffee-growing communities around the world."*

Coffee Kids
207 Wickenden Street
Providence, RI 20903
(800) 334-9099

⊸ PURPOSE ⊱
Preserve the integrity of the physical
buildings; expand knowledge of the eighteenth century

⊸ ACTIVITIES ⊱
Restoration; renovation; opening museums and
circulating collections to museums throughout the country

⊸ GIFTS ⊱
Catalog of reproductions: furniture, dinnerware,
mirrors, rugs, candlesticks, pewter, toys, books, linens,
jewelry, bedspreads, stemware, lanterns

*"The oldest and largest museum
reproductions program in the country"*

Colonial Williamsburg Foundation
P.O. Box 3532
Williamsburg, VA 23187-3532
(800) 446-9240

◄ PURPOSE ►

Save endangered rain forests,
marine and other threatened ecosystems

◄ ACTIVITIES ►

Identify wilderness areas of urgent conservation
priority; research; endangered species recovery; develop models
for sustainable harvesting of rain forest products; ecotourism

◄ GIFTS ►

T-shirts, sweatshirts,
notecards, posters, books, totes

"A future in jeopardy"

Conservation International
1015 18th Street NW, Suite 1000
Washington, DC 20036
(202) 429-5660

CONSERVATION TREATY SUPPORT FUND

⊸ PURPOSE ⊸
Promote awareness and understanding
of conservation treaties and their goals

⊸ ACTIVITIES ⊸
Support the Convention on International Trade
in Endangered Species (CITES), the Wetlands Treaty and
the major international conservation agreements

⊸ GIFTS ⊸
CITES Jr. Patrol
coloring books, posters, videos

*"Supporting international treaties
to conserve wild natural resources"*

Conservation Treaty Support Fund
3705 Cardiff Road
Chevy Chase, MD 20815
(301) 654-3150

COORS FOUNDATION FOR FAMILY LITERACY

⊰ PURPOSE ⊱
Promote literacy

⊰ ACTIVITIES ⊱
Teaching adults to read;
training literacy tutors

⊰ GIFTS ⊱
Books

"Literacy. Pass it on."

Coors Foundation for
Family Literacy
P.O. Box 46666
Denver, CO 80201
(800) 525-0308

COROLLA WILD HORSE FUND

⊸ PURPOSE ⊱
Protection of wild horses in
Currituck County, NC

⊸ ACTIVITIES ⊱
Media campaigns, public education,
Wild Horse Sanctuary

⊸ GIFTS ⊱
T-shirts, posters,
bookmarks

"Save the Wild Horses."

Corolla Wild Horse Fund
P.O. Box 361
Corolla, NC 27927

THE COSTEAU SOCIETY

⊸ PURPOSE ⊶
Protect and improve the quality of life
for present and future generations

⊸ ACTIVITIES ⊶
Education, ocean research, conservation projects;
develop new technology to study and
protect nature; filmmaking

⊸ GIFTS ⊶
Catalog: clothing, books, videos, art prints,
posters, soundtracks, calendars, totes

"People protect what they love."

The Costeau Society
870 Greenbrier Circle, Suite 402
Chesapeake, VA 23320
(804) 523-9335

CULTURAL SURVIVAL

⊸ PURPOSE ⊷
Advocate the rights of native
peoples and ethnic minorities worldwide

⊸ ACTIVITIES ⊷
Managing natural resources, participating in
the market economy, securing land rights, research,
public policy, education, publications

⊸ GIFTS ⊷
Catalog: body care products, books, posters, calendars,
trays, notecards, toys, T-shirts, rain forest products

*"Join the BUYcott. Buy products
that support standing forests."*

Cultural Survival
53A Church Street
Cambridge, MA 02138
(617) 495-2562

DEFENDERS OF WILDLIFE

⊸ PURPOSE ⊸
Conservation of all forms of wildlife

⊸ ACTIVITIES ⊸
Refuge support and reform, activist
network, litigation, legislation, education

⊸ GIFTS ⊸
Posters, postcards, notecards, greeting cards,
books, puzzles, T-shirts, sweatshirts,
sweatpants, sweatjackets, caps, neckties, puppets,
educational games, mugs, totes, keychains,
backpacks, suncatchers, jewelry

*"Making the world a safe place for wildlife
makes for a better world."*

Defenders of Wildlife
1244 19th Street NW
Washington, DC 20036
(202) 659-9510

DELAWARE VALLEY RAPTOR CENTER

⊸ PURPOSE ⊶
Conservation of birds of prey

⊸ ACTIVITIES ⊶
Treatment, rehabilitation and return to the wild
of injured, ill and orphaned raptors; public education

⊸ GIFTS ⊶
Adoption program: adoption certificate, color
photo of the bird sponsored, fact sheet, decal & sticker, DVRC
journal, starting at $15; T-shirts, sweatshirts, notecards

"The time has come to mother nature."

Delaware Valley Raptor Center
R.D. 2 Box 9335
Milford, PA 18337
(717) 296-6025

⌐ PURPOSE ⌐

Rescue unwanted dogs; supply hearing
and companion dogs to the hearing impaired

⌐ ACTIVITIES ⌐

Choosing and testing dogs from adoption
shelters; intensive training of the dogs and the
recipients; dog placement and follow-up

⌐ GIFTS ⌐

Sponsor a Hearing Dog: an article will appear in
the newspaper when the dog is placed, photo, letters from
the organization and the recipient of the dog; T-shirts,
sweatshirts, windbreakers, caps, pins, notecards

"To rescue unwanted dogs and give the gift of hearing"

Dogs for the Deaf, Inc.
10175 Wheeler Road
Central Point, OR 97502
(503) 826-9220

EARTHSAVE

⊸ PURPOSE ⊱

Educate and empower people
concerning the dietary link to environmental
and personal health

⊸ ACTIVITIES ⊱

Publishes and distributes environmental reports,
newsletters, books, video tapes and a catalog; sponsors
the Youth For Environmental Sanity (YES!)
Tour; summer camps and river rafting retreats;
Kinship With Life workshops

⊸ GIFTS ⊱

Catalog: books, videos, audios

*"The healthiest way to eat can also be the most economical, the
most compassionate and the least destructive for the planet as a whole."*

EarthSave
706 Frederick Street
Santa Cruz, CA 95062
(800) DNA-DO IT

EARTHSEA INSTITUTE

⊸ PURPOSE ⊱
Help single individuals have an
impact on global concerns

⊸ ACTIVITIES ⊱
Tree Life Connection tree plantings;
efforts to preserve Antarctica in its pristine state

⊸ GIFTS ⊱
Tree Plantings: certificate, card,
color photo of the site (in the California
Cosumnes River Preserve), $20

"The Gift of a Tree"

EarthSea Institute
P.O. Box 2164
Sausalito, CA 94966
(800) 326-6575 ♦ (415) 331-7060

⊸ PURPOSE ⊱

Expose and stop animal abuse and
other destructive impacts of factory farming

⊸ ACTIVITIES ⊱

The Great American Meatout,
Veal Ban Day, World Farm Animals Day,
Industry Watch, Farm Ed, publications

⊸ GIFTS ⊱

Books, videos, T-shirts

"Fight factory farming!"

Farm Animal Reform Movement (FARM)
P.O. Box 30654
Bethesda, MD 20897-1425
(301) 530-1737

⊸ PURPOSE ⊱

Save the lives of abused farm animals;
compel livestock facilities to adopt humane
care practices; vegetarian education

⊸ ACTIVITIES ⊱

Rescue animals from brutal factory farm
conditions; shelter and feed the animals at the Sanctuary

⊸ GIFTS ⊱

Adopt A Farm Animal: framed color photo of the
adopted animal, an adoption card, sponsorship booklet, regular
progress reports of the animal, $6-$40 per month depending
on type of farm animal chosen; Catalog: T-shirts,
posters, prints, notecards, books

"Be a farm animal friend!"

Farm Sanctuary
P.O. Box 150
Watkins Glen, NY 14891
(607) 583-2225

FLORIDA AUDUBON SOCIETY

⊸ PURPOSE ⊶
Conservation of birds of prey

⊸ ACTIVITIES ⊶
Treat, rehabilitate and release eagles, hawks and owls
that come to the center from all over the state (The birds
may be the victims of gunshot wounds, poisoning, power
line collisions and other injuries or health problems.);
maintain a permanent education center

⊸ GIFTS ⊶
Adopt-A-Bird: a color photo, biography of the bird
and species information, a personalized
adoption certificate, newsletter subscription, $20-$30

"Save these magnificent and majestic birds."

Florida Audubon Society
Center for Birds of Prey
460 HWY 436, Suite 200
Casselberry, FL 32707
(800) 874-BIRD

FOOD FIRST

⊸ PURPOSE ⊱

Bring about democratic social
change that can bring an end to hunger

⊸ ACTIVITIES ⊱

Publications; research; stop projects that
threaten to destroy the environment; promote
agrarian reform

⊸ GIFTS ⊱

Books, postcards,
T-shirts

"Hunger is not the human condition."

FOOD FIRST
Institute for Food and Development Policy
145 Ninth Street
San Francisco, CA 94103

FRIENDS OF ANIMALS

⊸ PURPOSE ⊶
Reduce and eliminate animal suffering
wherever it exists

⊸ ACTIVITIES ⊶
Low-cost nationwide spay/alter programs;
enlisting public and legislative support for wildlife
protection laws; investigating and exposing
cruel, abusive practices; education

⊸ GIFTS ⊶
Clothing, books

*"Education to establish a compassionate
ethic in the treatment of animals by humans"*

Friends of Animals
P.O. Box 1244
Norwalk, CT 06856
(203) 866-5223

FRIENDS OF THE AUSTRALIAN KOALA FOUNDATION

⌐ PURPOSE ⌐

Conservation of the
Australian koala and its habitat

⌐ ACTIVITIES ⌐

Care of sick and injured koalas,
planting koala food trees, research, education

⌐ GIFTS ⌐

Catalog: cards, T-shirts, mugs,
chocolates, jewelry, children's wear, posters, toys

*"The conservation of the koala and its
habitat is of global significance."*

Friends of the Australian Koala Foundation
50 West 29th Street, Suite 9W
New York, NY 10001
(212) 779-0700

FRIENDS OF THE EARTH

⊸ PURPOSE ⊱
Preserve our Earth

⊸ ACTIVITIES ⊱
Saving the ozone layer, ending tropical
deforestation, fighting global warming,
protecting the oceans, ending nuclear
weapons production

⊸ GIFTS ⊱
T-shirts, posters, notecards,
calendars, books

"Help the Earth fight back."

Friends of the Earth
218 D Street, SE
Washington, DC 20003
(202) 544-2600

FRIENDS OF THE RIVER

⊣ PURPOSE ⊢
Preserve, protect and restore
rivers, streams and their watersheds

⊣ ACTIVITIES ⊢
Generate political, legal and educational
support for river protection; sponsor river trips

⊣ GIFTS ⊢
T-shirts, rafting trips

"Our rivers need more friends."

Friends of the River
909 12th Street #207
Sacramento, CA 95814
(916) 442-3155

**FRIENDS OF
THE SEA LION**

◄ PURPOSE ►
Conservation of sea lions and
seals of Orange County, California

◄ ACTIVITIES ►
Rescue, rehabilitation, research, education

◄ GIFTS ►
Adopt A Seal or Sea Lion: adoption
certificate, choose the animal's name, visitation anytime,
attendance at the animal's release, $100;
Christmas cards, T-shirts

"Every environment is a unique crucible of living species."

Friends of the Sea Lion
Marine Mammal Center
20612 Laguna Canyon Road
Laguna Beach, CA 92651
(714) 494-3050

FRIENDS OF THE
SEA OTTER

⊰ PURPOSE ⊱

Aid in the protection and maintenance of a healthy
population of the southern sea otter and its nearshore marine
habitat along the California coast

⊰ ACTIVITIES ⊱

Educational programs; reducing threats to the otters
from oil spills, coastal pollution, illegal gill netting and
malicious killings; achieving state bans
on gill netting; Sea Otter Center

⊰ GIFTS ⊱

T-shirts, sweatshirts, neckties, jewelry, books, wind chimes,
totes, rubber stamps, prints, calendars, stationery, key rings,
giftwrap, toys, serving trays, holiday cards, videos

"The sea otter...a threatened species"

Friends of the Sea Otter
P.O. Box 221220
Carmel, CA 93922
(408) 625-3290

FRIENDS OF THE VIETNAM VETERANS MEMORIAL

⌐ PURPOSE ⌐

Maintain the Vietnam Veterans Memorial as the nation's
primary symbol of honor for Vietnam veterans and their families
and preserve its historical legacy

⌐ ACTIVITIES ⌐

Assist visitors at the Memorial; place flowers for those who cannot visit;
fulfill name rubbing requests; In Touch program to locate those who
knew someone whose name is inscribed on the
Memorial; help veterans find each other

⌐ GIFTS ⌐

Books, bronze statues, granite name engravings, videos,
postcards, T-shirts, sweatshirts, notecards, pins, posters, prints

"To honor those who served"

Friends of the Vietnam Veterans Memorial
2030 Clarendon Boulevard, Suite 412
Arlington, VA 22201
(202) 628-0726

**THE FUND
FOR ANIMALS**

⊷ PURPOSE ⊷
Foster humane conduct toward animals and
relieve animal suffering everywhere

⊷ ACTIVITIES ⊷
Animal rescue and protection,
humane education, spaying programs,
anti-hunting strategies

⊷ GIFTS ⊷
T-shirts, books

"Support your right to arm bears."

The Fund for Animals
200 West 57th Street
New York, NY 10019
(212) 246-2096

GLOBAL TOMORROW COALITION

⊸ PURPOSE ⊷
Assure a more sustainable,
equitable, productive and humane global future

⊸ ACTIVITIES ⊷
International assemblies, forums, congressional
briefings, global town meetings, teacher-training workshops

⊸ GIFTS ⊷
Stationery, key chains, mugs, visors,
paperweights, pens, shoelaces, headbands, T-shirts, books

"Work for a Sustainable Future."

Global Tomorrow Coalition
1325 G Street, N.W., Suite 1010
Washington, DC 20005-3104
(202) 628-4016

GRAND CANYON TRUST

⊸ PURPOSE ⊷
Preservation, protection and wise
management of the public lands, water, wildlife and
other natural resources of the Grand Canyon
and the Colorado Plateau

⊸ ACTIVITIES ⊷
Conduct research and develop recommendations
concerning specific issues affecting the
natural resources of the Colorado Plateau

⊸ GIFTS ⊷
T-shirts, books, calendars

*"Providing a long term vision for
the Colorado Plateau"*

Grand Canyon Trust
The Homestead
Route 4, Box 718
Flagstaff, AZ 86001
(602) 774-7488

GREAT BEAR FOUNDATION

⊷ PURPOSE ⊶

Preservation of each of the
Earth's eight species of bears

⊷ ACTIVITIES ⊶

Education, legislation, reimbursement to
ranchers of livestock killed by grizzly bears, information
sharing internationally, legal defense
support, grants, publications

⊷ GIFTS ⊶

Books, T-shirts, sweatshirts, postcards,
pins, belt buckles, belts, caps, posters

*"Grizzlies need lots of wide open spaces and
are losing them even in Alaska."*

Great Bear Foundation
P.O. Box 2699
Missoula, MT 59806
(406) 721-3009

GREATER LOS ANGELES ZOO ASSOCIATION

⊰ PURPOSE ⊱
Preserve the diversity of life

⊰ ACTIVITIES ⊱
Specialized breeding programs,
habitat preservation, study and protection of
endangered species in the wild

⊰ GIFTS ⊱
Animal sponsorship: certificate, *Zoo View*
magazine, gifts of $75 or more will be
recognized in the Donor Showcase for
one year, starting at $25

Greater Los Angeles Zoo Association
5333 Zoo Drive
Los Angeles, CA 90027-1498
(213) 664-1100

GREAT OLD BROADS FOR WILDERNESS

⊸ PURPOSE ⊱
Protection and growth of the
National Wilderness Preservation System

⊸ ACTIVITIES ⊱
Push for passage of critical legislation
through letter writing, parades, protests and
demonstrations; annual conference

⊸ GIFTS ⊱
T-shirts

"Wise women protecting Wilderness"

Great Old Broads for Wilderness
P.O. Box 520307
Salt Lake City, UT 84152-0307
(801) 539-8208

⊰ PURPOSE ⊱

Preserve our environment and
protect the creatures that share our planet

⊰ ACTIVITIES ⊱

Positive, non-violent action to stop
pollution, the slaughter of whales and dolphins,
the spread of nuclear weapons, global warming
and the destruction of the ozone layer

⊰ GIFTS ⊱

Catalog: clothing, totes, jewelry, watches,
mugs, calendars, posters, rain forest soaps, toys,
puzzles, games, notecards, stationery,
giftwrap, books, key rings

"Stepping lightly on the Earth"

Greenpeace
P.O. Box 77048
San Francisco, CA 94107-0048
(800) 456-4029

⤙ PURPOSE ⤚
Eliminate poverty housing from the world

⤙ ACTIVITIES ⤚
Builds and rehabilitates homes with
the help of the homeowners and volunteers

⤙ GIFTS ⤚
Catalog: T-shirts, sweatshirts, posters,
books, totes, videos, audios,
notecards, postcards

"Building around the world"

Habitat for Humanity International
121 Habitat Street
Americus, GA 31709-3498
(912) 924-6935

HawkWatch International

⊸ Purpose ⊸

Monitor and preserve our birds of prey,
their habitats and the global environment

⊸ Activities ⊸

Discovering new raptor flyways, conducting migration
counts, banding programs, sponsoring training of young
field biologists, environmental education programs

⊸ Gifts ⊸

Adopt-A-Hawk: personalized adoption certificate,
periodic update, color photo, fact sheet, membership in
HawkWatch International, $25; books, T-shirts, etc.

"Preserving raptors and our environment"

HawkWatch International
P.O. Box 35706
Albuquerque, NM 87176-5706
(800) 726-HAWK

⊸ PURPOSE ⊱

Alleviate world hunger and poverty by
enabling families to produce their own food and income

⊸ ACTIVITIES ⊱

Provides groups of rural families with gifts of livestock
and training in animal husbandry, regenerative agricultural
methods, and community development; educates
on the causes of hunger and poverty

⊸ GIFTS ⊱

T-shirts, sweatshirts, caps, postcards

"Good neighbor to the world"

Heifer Project International
1015 South Louisiana
P.O. Box 808
Little Rock, AR 72203
(800) 422-0474

THE HUMANE FARMING ASSOCIATION

⊸ PURPOSE ⊢
Protect consumers from the dangerous
misuse of chemicals in food production; eliminate
the suffering to which farm animals are subjected

⊸ ACTIVITIES ⊢
Public education, legislation, the National
Veal Boycott, the Campaign Against Factory Farming

⊸ GIFTS ⊢
T-shirts, coloring books,
greeting cards, posters

"Farm animals need protection too."

The Humane Farming Association
P.O. Box 3577
San Rafael, CA 94912-8902
(415) 771-CALF

THE HUMANE SOCIETY OF THE UNITED STATES

⊸ PURPOSE ⊶

Protection of animals through
investigative, legal, educational and legislative means

⊸ ACTIVITIES ⊶

Reducing the overbreeding of dogs and cats;
eliminating suffering of animals used in research;
stopping sport hunting; improving conditions
in zoos, shelters, pet stores, kennels and circuses

⊸ GIFTS ⊶

Catalog: T-shirts, totes, books,
notecards, greeting cards, posters

"Animals...It's their world too!"

The Humane Society of the United States
2100 L Street, NW
Washington, DC 20037
(202) 452-1100

~ PURPOSE ~
Conserve and protect primates

~ ACTIVITIES ~
Create and control national parks and
sanctuaries; control of primate hunting, trapping
and sale; education; anti-poaching patrols

~ GIFTS ~
T-shirts, sweatshirts, greeting cards

"Illegal wildlife trade is growing."

International Primate Protection League
P.O. Box 766
Summerville, SC 29484
(803) 871-2280

INTERNATIONAL SOCIETY FOR ENDANGERED CATS

⭐ Purpose ⭐
Save wild cat species from extinction

⭐ Activities ⭐
Acquiring cats for breeding;
building breeding facilities; research

⭐ Gifts ⭐
T-shirts, mugs, notecards,
jewelry, ceramic figures

"Cats <u>don't</u> have nine lives!"

International Society for Endangered Cats
4638 Winterset Drive
Columbus, OH 43220
(614) 451-4460

⤙ Purpose ⤚
Promote professional networking and
continuing education in wildlife rehabilitation, as
well as a standardized approach to wildlife care

⤙ Activities ⤚
Annual conference, publications,
wildlife information hotline,
certified skills seminars

⤙ Gifts ⤚
T-shirts, totes, notecards

"Better care through shared knowledge..."

International Wildlife Rehabilitation Council
4437 Central Place, Suite B-4
Suisun, CA 94585
(707) 864-1761

KEEP AMERICA BEAUTIFUL

⊸ PURPOSE ⊷
Improve waste handling
practices in American communities

⊸ ACTIVITIES ⊷
Public education, training
of community leaders, publications

⊸ GIFTS ⊷
Books, sweatshirts, videos, mugs, pins

"Waste in place"

Keep America Beautiful
9 West Broad Street
Stamford, CT 06902
(203) 323-8987

⊰ PURPOSE ⊱
Educate; empower and inspire
children to protect the environment

⊰ ACTIVITIES ⊱
15,000 Kids for Saving Earth Clubs in
34 countries work on Earth-saving projects.

⊰ GIFTS ⊱
T-shirts, totes, lunch
bags, mugs, pins, music, books

"The Earth is my home."

Kids for Saving Earth
P.O. Box 47247
Plymouth, MN 55447-0247
(612) 525-0002

M.D. ANDERSON CANCER CENTER

⮜ PURPOSE ⮞
Meet the educational, recreational
and emotional needs of cancer patients

⮜ ACTIVITIES ⮞
Summer camps for young cancer patients,
amputee ski trips, prosthetic devices, weekly pediatric parties,
special events and outings, college and graduate scholarships,
materials for the Patient/Family Library

⮜ GIFTS ⮞
Christmas cards, ornaments, notecards, T-shirts,
sweatshirts, gift bags designed by young cancer patients

"Enjoy these products and help young cancer patients."

M.D. Anderson Cancer Center
Children's Christmas Card Project
P.O. Box 301435
Houston, TX 77250-1435
(800) 231-1580

THE MEXICAN WOLF COALITION OF TEXAS

◄ PURPOSE ►

Save the Mexican wolf from extinction

◄ ACTIVITIES ►

Provide public education on the plight
of the Mexican wolf; assist in reintroduction efforts
of the Mexican wolf into its native habitat in
Texas and other parts of the Southwest

◄ GIFTS ►

T-shirts

"Return the Mexican wolf to the wild."

The Mexican Wolf Coalition of Texas
P.O. Box 851224
Richardson, TX 75085-1224
(713) 443-0012

THE MOUNTAIN LION FOUNDATION

⚊ PURPOSE ⚊

Ensure protection and survival for
American lions and their wilderness homes

⚊ ACTIVITIES ⚊

Monitor ongoing research and habitat studies;
identify critical habitat areas; public education; work
to ban trophy hunting; publications

⚊ GIFTS ⚊

Adopt-A-Lion: adoption certificate with a photo
of your lion, fact sheets, quarterly updates, $25;
books, bolo ties, T-shirts, totes, posters,
greeting cards, pins, notecards, mugs, videos

*"The American lion...let's preserve our
rich natural heritage."*

The Mountain Lion Foundation
P.O. Box 1896
Sacramento, CA 95812
(916) 442-2666

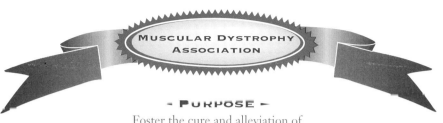

MUSCULAR DYSTROPHY ASSOCIATION

⊸ PURPOSE ⊱

Foster the cure and alleviation of
muscular dystrophy and other neuromuscular diseases

⊸ ACTIVITIES ⊱

Patient and community services,
research, education

⊸ GIFTS ⊱

Calendars

*"MDA conducts the
Jerry Lewis Labor Day Telethon."*

Muscular Dystrophy Association
P.O. Box 1494
New York, NY 10113-1930
(212) 586-0808

NATIONAL ARCHIVES TRUST FUND

⤙ PURPOSE ⤚

Preserve the important papers of the American
nation: the Declaration of Independence, the Constitution,
the Bill of Rights, census records, military service
files, maps, photographs, film

⤙ ACTIVITIES ⤚

Operating record centers, archives and
Presidential libraries; genealogy workshops, exhibitions

⤙ GIFTS ⤚

Catalog: sculptures, books, bookends, family trees,
ceramics, White House china reproductions, T-shirts, sweatshirts,
notecards, scarves, toys, games, ornaments

"These rich stores of materials are available to all."

National Archives Trust Fund
P.O. Box 100793
Atlanta, GA 30384
(800) 788-6282

⊰ PURPOSE ⊱

Ensure that services are available to all
who are deaf or hard-of-hearing so that they
may achieve their full potential

⊰ ACTIVITIES ⊱

Influencing legislation; sponsoring youth
programs, conferences and the Miss Deaf America
competition; referrals, education

⊰ GIFTS ⊱

Catalog: books, games, videos, rubber
stamps, key chains, totes, Christmas cards,
stationery, notecards and pads

"You don't need words to communicate."

National Association of the Deaf Bookstore
814 Thayer Avenue
Silver Spring, MD 20910
(301) 587-6282

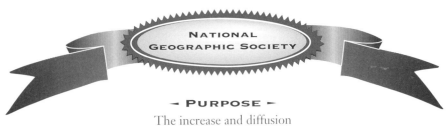

NATIONAL GEOGRAPHIC SOCIETY

⊸ PURPOSE ⊱
The increase and diffusion
of geographic knowledge

⊸ ACTIVITIES ⊱
Research and exploration, geography education
in the classroom, mapmaking, Explorer's Hall museum,
magazines, books, television programming

⊸ GIFTS ⊱
Catalog: books, videos, calendars,
globes, maps, games, magazine subscriptions

"Making sense of where we are"

National Geographic Society
P.O. Box 2118
Washington, DC 20013-2118
(800) 638-4077

NATIONAL MUSEUM OF WOMEN IN THE ARTS

⊸ PURPOSE ⊷

A forum for greater awareness of the outstanding
achievements by women in the visual and performing arts

⊸ ACTIVITIES ⊷

Exhibitions, publications, educational programs,
varied performances, state outreach programs; the Library and
Research Center with the world's most comprehensive
source of information about women artists

⊸ GIFTS ⊷

Books, posters, notecards,
sweatshirts, jewelry, music by women, scarves

"Highlighting the achievements of women artists"

National Museum of Women in the Arts
1250 New York Avenue, NW
Washington, DC 20005-3920
(202) 783-5000

⌐ Purpose ⌐
Protect and improve the
quality of our national park system

⌐ Activities ⌐
Research, education, stopping archaeological
vandalism, reintroducing the wolf to Yellowstone,
efforts to limit park aircraft overflights

⌐ Gifts ⌐
Catalog: T-shirts, sweatshirts, mugs, jewelry,
posters, videos, calendars, totes, stuffed bears, jackets,
caps, puzzles, luggage, Swiss army knives

"Wild about the parks"

National Parks and Conservation Association
1776 Massachusetts Avenue, NW
Washington, DC 20036
(800) NAT-PARK

THE NATIONAL STUDENT CAMPAIGN AGAINST HUNGER & HOMELESSNESS

⊷ PURPOSE ⊷
Fight hunger and homelessness in the
United States and around the world

⊷ ACTIVITIES ⊷
Assist individuals and groups leading locally-initiated
projects and Campaign-sponsored programs; Hunger and
Homelessness Week; Hunger Cleanup; a national
conference; food salvage

⊷ GIFTS ⊷
T-shirts

"Students making a difference"

The National Student Campaign
Against Hunger and Homelessness
29 Temple Place
Boston, MA 02111
(617) 292-4823

⊰ PURPOSE ⊱
Encourage the conservation and use of
native plants in North American landscapes

⊰ ACTIVITIES ⊱
Education, research, festivals,
workshops, landscaping seminars

⊰ GIFTS ⊱
Catalog: books, T-shirts, sweatshirts,
chairs, trays, notecards, mugs, pins

"The difference is WILD!"

National Wildflower Research Center
2600 FM 973 North
Austin, TX 78725-4201
(512) 929-0513

⊸ Purpose ⊷
Educate the public to conserve natural
resources and protect the environment

⊸ Activities ⊷
Institute for Wildlife Research, Wildlife Camps,
outdoor discovery vacations, publications, award programs,
conservation internships, Wildlife Week

⊸ Gifts ⊷
Catalog: clothing, jewelry, books, prints, mugs, bird
feeders, stationery, toys, educational kits and games, posters, sculptures,
Rainforest Crunch, housewares, videos, audios, giftwrap, totes

"Working for the nature of tomorrow"

National Wildlife Federation
1400 16th Street, NW
Washington, DC 20036-2266
(800) 432-6564

⊸ PURPOSE ⊷

"To force the nuclear industry and
government to reduce radioactive contamination
of Indian land and people"

⊸ ACTIVITIES ⊷

Public education, cultural responsibility,
citizen activism, legal intervention, independent analysis,
resource identification and coordination

⊸ GIFTS ⊷

T-shirts, caps (beaded on request), jackets,
duffel bags, posters, postcards

"We are the resistance. . . leave uranium in the ground."

Native Americans for a Clean Environment
P.O. Box 1671
Tahlequah, OK 74465
(918) 458-4322

NATURAL RESOURCES DEFENSE COUNCIL

⊸ PURPOSE ⊱

Protect the environment and natural
resources for the general welfare of the public

⊸ ACTIVITIES ⊱

Education, litigation, influencing legislation,
scientific research; efforts to reduce acid rain, ozone depletion,
global warming, pollution and use of nuclear weapons

⊸ GIFTS ⊱

Books, T-shirts, cassette
tape of rain forest sounds

*"Protecting the environment with
the power of law, science and people"*

Natural Resources Defense Council
40 West 20th Street
New York, NY 10011
(212) 727-2700

⊸ PURPOSE ⊷
Preserve plants, animals and natural
communities by protecting the places they need to survive

⊸ ACTIVITIES ⊷
Identifying rare species, acquiring
habitats, establishing and managing preserves

⊸ GIFTS ⊷
Adopt-an-Acre: honorary land deed, quarterly
reports from local conservation group about activities affecting
your adopted acreage, $35 plus $2.50 shipping and handling;
mugs, T-shirts, totes, ties, sweatshirts, caps, books, cards

"Conservation through private action"

Nature Conservancy
1815 North Lynn Street
Arlington, VA 22209
(800) 628-6860, Adopt-an Acre only
(703) 841-8747

⊸ PURPOSE ⊷

End the exploitation and suffering of animals

⊸ ACTIVITIES ⊷

Public school education and community outreach;
cruelty-free guides; sanctuary support for animals rescued from labs;
conferences; legislative campaigns; volunteers' projects

⊸ GIFTS ⊷

T-shirts, books, greeting cards

*"The greatness of a nation and its moral progress can be
judged by the way its animals are treated."* (Gandhi)

New England Anti-Vivisection Society
333 Washington Street, Suite 850
Boston, MA 02108
(617) 523-6020

**NEW ENGLAND
WILD FLOWER SOCIETY**

⊸ PURPOSE ⊱
Promote the conservation of
temperate North American plants

⊸ ACTIVITIES ⊱
Operation of the botanical garden,
Garden in the Woods; courses, lectures, tours, conferences,
field trips, research, advocacy; a regional conservation
program to protect rare plants in the United States

⊸ GIFTS ⊱
Books, garden ornaments, gifts
related to nature and plants

"New England Plant Conservation"

New England Wild Flower Society
180 Hemenway Road
Framingham, MA 01701-2699
(617) 237-4924 ◆ (508) 877-7630

THE NEW YORK TURTLE & TORTOISE SOCIETY

⊸ PURPOSE ⊹

Conservation and preservation of turtle and
tortoise habitats and the promotion of proper captive
propagation and husbandry

⊸ ACTIVITIES ⊹

Education, publications, seminars, Annual Turtle
and Photography Show, field trips, care and rehabilitation
of injured wild turtles

⊸ GIFTS ⊹

Books, T-shirts, games

"Leave wild turtles in the wild."

The New York Turtle and Tortoise Society
163 Amsterdam Avenue, Suite 365
New York, NY 10023
(212) 459-4803

NEW YORK ZOOLOGICAL SOCIETY

⊸ PURPOSE ⊸

Assure the survival of endangered species

⊸ ACTIVITIES ⊸

Conservation, education, research

⊸ GIFTS ⊸

Sponsor-A-Species: adoption
certificate, photo, starting at $250

*"You can help assure
the survival of endangered species."*

New York Zoological Society
Bronx Zoo
Bronx, NY 10460
(212) 220-5090

⊰ PURPOSE ⊱
Increase the populations of the
three species of bluebirds on this continent

⊰ ACTIVITIES ⊱
Research, education, media campaigns

⊰ GIFTS ⊱
Catalog: Christmas cards, notecards, postcards, art prints,
books, nesting boxes, bluebird feeders, T-shirts, sweatshirts,
caps, jewelry, coloring books, totes, trivets, giftwrap

"Where have all the bluebirds gone?"

The North American Bluebird Society
Box 6295
Silver Spring, MD 20916-6295

⊸ PURPOSE ⊸

Fund self-help development and disaster relief in
poor countries in Africa, Asia, Latin America and the Caribbean

⊸ ACTIVITIES ⊸

Support grassroots organizations whose efforts increase
food production, education and trade to poor people throughout
the world; education on the root causes of hunger and poverty

⊸ GIFTS ⊸

Catalog: books, jewelry, housewares, clothing,
wood sculptures, foods, toys, musical instruments,
baskets, notecards

"Self-help around the world"

Oxfam America
P.O. Box 821
Lewiston, ME 04240
(800) 639-2141

⊱ PURPOSE ⊰

Education about conservation issues
of marine mammals and their ocean environment

⊱ ACTIVITIES ⊰

Conservation, research,
experiential learning programs, publications

⊱ GIFTS ⊰

Adopt-A-Whale: adoption certificate, photo,
letter of whale's latest activities, map of the whale's location
when last sighted, newsletter, $25

"...Because extinction is forever."

Pacific Whale Foundation
101 North Kihei Road
Kihei, Maui, HI 96753
(808) 879-8860

⌐ PURPOSE ⌐

Improve the care, quality of life and
survival rate of children with malignant diseases

⌐ ACTIVITIES ⌐

Research

⌐ GIFTS ⌐

Holiday greeting cards designed by children
who benefit directly from the Foundation, notecards,
sweatshirts, T-shirts, mugs

"Children's Hospital of Orange County"

The Pediatric Cancer Research Foundation
P.O. Box 1076
Orange, CA 92668-0076
(714) 532-8692

PELICAN MAN'S BIRD SANCTUARY

⤝ PURPOSE ⤞

Rescue and rehabilitation of injured birds

⤝ ACTIVITIES ⤞

Operate the sanctuary which
houses, feeds and gives medical care

⤝ GIFTS ⤞

Adopt-A-Pelican: choose a pelican or other
bird (heron, crane, egret, owl, vulture) to receive a
presentation folder with a color photo and
a case history of your bird, $25

"I tend the hurt and feed the hungry."

Pelican Man's Bird Sanctuary, Inc.
P.O. Box 2648
Sarasota, FL 34230
(813) 955-2266

THE PIERPONT MORGAN LIBRARY

⊰ PURPOSE ⊱
Scholarly research and museum

⊰ ACTIVITIES ⊱
Museum operation,
publications, concerts, lectures, exhibitions

⊰ GIFTS ⊱
Catalog: greeting cards,
books, totes, jewelry

"Pierpont Morgan's gift to the American people"

The Pierpont Morgan Library
29 East 36th Street
New York, NY 10016
(212) 685-0008

⊰ PURPOSE ⊱

Promote the scientific exploration of our
solar system and the search for extraterrestrial life

⊰ ACTIVITIES ⊱

Conferences of scientists and engineers,
public events, educators' workshops, publications, research,
scholarships, grants

⊰ GIFTS ⊱

Catalog: books, notecards, watches, posters,
videos, slides, puzzles, T-shirts, sweatshirts, pins, key rings,
mugs, calendars, totes, pencils

"If you are interested in the future of planetary exploration..."

The Planetary Society
65 North Catalina Avenue
Pasadena, CA 91106
(818) 793-1675

PRAIRIE DOG RESCUE

⊣ PURPOSE ⊢
Preservation of prairie dogs in their natural habitat

⊣ ACTIVITIES ⊢
Demonstrations; letter-writing and phone calls
whenever public pressure is called for; education; prairie dog
rescue and relocation; legal issues

⊣ GIFTS ⊢
Jewelry, T-shirts, posters, postcards, paperweights

"Prairie dogs have been reduced by 90% since 1900."

Prairie Dog Rescue, Inc.
P.O. Box 8054
Englewood, CO 80110
(303) 266-3687

PROGRAMME
FOR BELIZE

⚊ PURPOSE ⚊

Link economic development and the
conservation of Belize's wildlife, forest and marine resources

⚊ ACTIVITIES ⚊

Holding land in trust for the people of Belize
to be utilized for natural history, archaeological tourism,
long-term scientific research and agro-forestry projects

⚊ GIFTS ⚊

Adopt-An-Acre, $50 or Investment Certificates,
$100: each includes a certificate, gift folder, thank you
letter, and newsletter; posters

"An opportunity for positive action"

Programme for Belize
P.O. Box 1088
Vineyard Haven, MA 02568
(800) 343-8009 ♦ (508) 693-0856

⊰ Purpose ⊱
Promote and protect the rights,
interests and well-being of all animals

⊰ Activities ⊱
Provide shelter, adoption and lost and found
services for companion animals; care for injured
and orphaned wildlife; education; legislation

⊰ Gifts ⊱
Catalog: T-shirts, sweatshirts, totes, mugs,
key tags, books, greeting cards, dog leashes

*"PAWS adoption program has placed
over 25,000 dogs and cats in permanent homes."*

Progressive Animal Welfare Society (PAWS)
P.O. Box 1037
Lynnwood, WA 98046
(206) 742-4142

⊸ PURPOSE ⊶

Support craft and agricultural cooperatives of
very low income people in Latin America to raise the
income and living standards of the producers

⊸ ACTIVITIES ⊶

Operate the Houston store and catalog
selling products from these cooperatives

⊸ GIFTS ⊶

Catalog: all-cotton clothing, jewelry,
greeting cards, housewares, foods, toys, books, music

"Hidden wealth: Ethnic treasures of the New World"

Pueblo to People
P.O. Box 2545
Houston, TX 77252-2545
(800) 843-5257

⊰ PURPOSE ⊱
Promote interest in the environment and
encourage enlightened conservation measures with a focus
on chemical contamination

⊰ ACTIVITIES ⊱
Publications; clearinghouse of
information for scientists and laymen

⊰ GIFTS ⊱
Books

"An association for the integrity of the environment"

Rachel Carson Council, Inc.
8940 Jones Mill Road
Chevy Chase, MD 20815
(301) 652-1877

⊰ PURPOSE ⊱
Convert America's abandoned
railroad corridors to trails for public use

⊰ ACTIVITIES ⊱
Public education, advocacy,
legislation, regulatory action, technical assistance

⊰ GIFTS ⊱
Books, calendars, greeting cards, flashlights,
water bottles, pins, mugs, totes, caps, T-shirts, jackets

"Restoring life to abandoned railroad corridors"

Rails to Trails Conservancy
1400 16th Street, NW
Washington, DC 20036
(202) 797-5400

⊸ PURPOSE ⊷

Save rain forests and educate the public
about why rain forests are so important as vital support
systems for the earth and its people

⊸ ACTIVITIES ⊷

Media campaigns: boycotting Burger King's
import of beef from rain forest areas; calling for
a ban on import of tropical timber

⊸ GIFTS ⊷

Protect-An-Acre (protect rain forests by supporting
Indian efforts for land title): certificate stating how many acres
you helped protect, what tribe you helped support, and where
they are located-$25 will protect 1,750 acres and $100 can
protect 7,000 acres; books, videos, T-shirts, posters, pins

"Promote rain forest awareness."

Rainforest Action Network
301 Broadway, Suite A
San Francisco, CA 94133
(415) 398-4404

RARE CENTER FOR TROPICAL CONSERVATION

⤙ PURPOSE ⤚
Preserve threatened wildlife and its habitats
(currently active in Latin America and the Caribbean)

⤙ ACTIVITIES ⤚
Environmental education, reserve
design evaluation, ecotourism guide training

⤙ GIFTS ⤚
Posters, T-shirts

*"Dedicated to the conservation of
endangered tropical wildlife and its habitats"*

RARE Center for Tropical Conservation
1529 Walnut Street
Philadelphia, PA 19102
(215) 568-0420

ROCKY MOUNTAIN
RAPTOR PROGRAM

⊸ PURPOSE ⊱

Provide medical care and rehabilitation to
injured birds of prey; environmental education to the public

⊸ ACTIVITIES ⊱

Feed, medicate and rehabilitate injured eagles,
hawks, falcons and owls for release back to the wild

⊸ GIFTS ⊱

Adopt-A-Raptor : certificate, photo of the bird, a Christmas
card, newsletter, updates on the bird's activities, starting at $15

*"Become personally involved in the care
of one of our raptor residents."*

Rocky Mountain Raptor Program
Colorado State University
Veterinary Teaching Hospital
300 West Drake
Fort Collins, CO 80523
(303) 491-0398

SAN FRANCISCO ZOO

⊸ PURPOSE ⊱
Promote global conservation through the
acquisition of threatened habitats around the world

⊸ ACTIVITIES ⊱
Acquire rain forest acreage in Costa Rica
and Belize to be managed by local conservationists

⊸ GIFTS ⊱
Adopt-An-Acre: honorary deed noting
the amount of acreage purchased and the country of location,
starting at $15.

*"Habitat destruction is the greatest
threat to wildlife today."*

San Francisco Zoo
Adopt-An-Acre
1 Zoo Road
San Francisco, CA 94132
(415) 753-7080

⊸ PURPOSE ⊸
Make lasting, positive differences
in the lives of disadvantaged children

⊸ ACTIVITIES ⊸
Prenatal care, birth-spacing education, family health,
early childhood development, teen counseling

⊸ GIFTS ⊸
Catalog: greeting cards, tree ornaments, giftwrap,
jewelry, toys, clothing, housewares, stationery, desk accessories,
totes, sculptures, puzzles

"Helping communities help themselves"

Save the Children
P.O. Box 166
Peru, IN 46970
(800) 833-3154

SAVE THE MANATEE CLUB

⫸ PURPOSE ⫷
Conserve Florida's state
marine mammal, the endangered manatee

⫸ ACTIVITIES ⫷
Lobbying for legislation;
public awareness; education; research

⫸ GIFTS ⫷
Adopt-A-Manatee: adoption certificate,
biography of an individual manatee, an underwater photo,
a manatee fact sheet; sweatshirts, aprons, mugs,
books, jewelry, figurines, duffle bags

"Save the Manatee."

Save the Manatee Club
Florida Audubon Society
500 N. Maitland Avenue, Suite 210
Maitland, FL 32751
(800) 432-JOIN

SAVE THE RAINFOREST

⊰ PURPOSE ⊱
Rain forest conservation

⊰ ACTIVITIES ⊱
Stimulating an environmental ethic at the
grassroots level; raising money for conservation projects
in countries too poor to finance them; education

⊰ GIFTS ⊱
Purchase an acre of the Rio Bravo
Children's Rainforest: certificate, $30

"Forgive the foreign debt of tropical rainforest countries."

Save the Rainforest
604 Jamie Street
Dodgeville, WI 53533
(608) 935-9435

SAVE-THE-REDWOODS LEAGUE

⊸ PURPOSE ⊱
Protect and conserve California's
Redwood forests in public parks

⊸ ACTIVITIES ⊱
Redwood land purchase,
education, park reforestation

⊸ GIFTS ⊱
Tree planting: gift notification card,
permanent record, $50; posters, postcards

"The state of California will match your donation."

Save-the-Redwoods League
114 Sansome Street, Room 605
San Francisco, CA 94104
(415) 362-2352

SAVE THE WHALES INTERNATIONAL

► PURPOSE ◄
Save whales and
their natural environment

► ACTIVITIES ◄
Promote a world-wide whaling ban,
confront whaling ships, ban driftnets

► GIFTS ◄
Adopt A Humpback Whale: adoption certificate,
color photo, Earthtrust newsletter, annual report, $40

"Join the whale-saving team!"

Save the Whales International
Earthtrust
25 Kaneohe Bay Drive #205
Kailua, HI 96734
(808) 254-2866

⊸ Purpose ⊷

Apply ecological concepts
to human interaction with the land

⊸ Activities ⊷

Curriculum guides for grades K-12

⊸ Gifts ⊷

Books, naturalist's tools, clothing, toys and
games about nature, cassettes of songs and stories

"Reaching for connections"

Schlitz Audubon Center
1111 East Brown Deer Road
Milwaukee, WI 53217-1999
(414) 352-2880

⊸ PURPOSE ⊱
Promote peace and
international understanding

⊸ ACTIVITIES ⊱
Organizes short-term, voluntary work
projects, called workcamps, in the USA and overseas

⊸ GIFTS ⊱
T-shirts, batiks

"International Peace: We work for it."

SCI International Voluntary Service
Route 2 Box 506
Crozet, VA 22932
(804) 823-1826

⊸ Purpose ⊹

Save sea turtles and other endangered
species through increased public awareness of
the problems faced by these animals

⊸ Activities ⊹

Slide presentations to schools, research field
projects, volunteer study groups, conservation

⊸ Gifts ⊹

T-shirts, sweatshirts,
silk scarves, puzzles, books

*"There are seven species of Sea Turtles...
all are endangered or threatened."*

Sea Turtle Center
11276 East Lime Kiln Road
Grass Valley, CA 95945
(916) 274-2427

SELFHELP CRAFTS OF THE WORLD

⊸ PURPOSE ⊷

Assist low-income people in developing
countries to earn a living by selling their handcrafts
in North America

⊸ ACTIVITIES ⊷

Free marketing and business services to
producer groups; insuring fair wages; operation
of retail shops

⊸ GIFTS ⊷

Baskets, clothing, jewelry, greeting cards, toys,
linens, stationery, housewares, totes, art objects,
desk accessories, crafts, ornaments, musical
instruments, wood carvings

"Jobs with dignity"

SELFHELP Crafts of the World
704 Main Street
P.O. Box 500
Akron, PA 17501-0500
(717) 859-4971

SERRV SELF-HELP HANDCRAFTS

⊸ PURPOSE ⊶

Promote the social and economic progress
of people in developing regions of the world by purchasing
and marketing their handcrafts in a just and direct manner

⊸ ACTIVITIES ⊶

Church and community groups purchase
SERRV products or receive them on consignment or
wholesale and market them in their local community

⊸ GIFTS ⊶

Catalog: jewelry, clothing, toys, musical instruments,
rugs, baskets, furniture, linens, notecards, wood carvings,
ornaments, greeting cards, holiday items, coffee

"Each item has been fashioned by human hands."

SERRV Self-Help Handcrafts
500 Main Street
P.O. Box 365
New Windsor, MD 21776-0365
(800) 423-0071

SHARE OUR STRENGTH

⊰ PURPOSE ⊱

Bring creative professionals from
a variety of fields together to help fight hunger

⊰ ACTIVITIES ⊱

Taste of the Nation benefit; program for
restaurants to salvage their leftover food; public education

⊰ GIFTS ⊱

Calendars, books

*"A nationwide network of creative
professionals fighting hunger"*

Share Our Strength
1511 K Street, NW, Suite 600
Washington, DC 20005
(800) 222-1767

⊰ PURPOSE ⊱
Preservation, protection and
enjoyment of the world environment

⊰ ACTIVITIES ⊱
Lobbying, public education,
publications, national and chapter outings

⊰ GIFTS ⊱
Catalog: notecards, clothing, totes, books,
mugs, calendars, stitchery kits, jewelry, posters, art prints,
toys, giftwrap, ornaments, greeting cards, wind-bells,
Swiss army knives, walking sticks, backpacks

"One hundred years of protecting nature"

Sierra Club
Sierra Club Store
730 Polk Street
San Francisco, CA 94109
(415) 776-2211

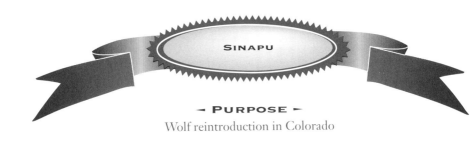

⤙ PURPOSE ⤚
Wolf reintroduction in Colorado

⤙ ACTIVITIES ⤚
Public education,
grass roots organizing, political action

⤙ GIFTS ⤚
Postcards

*"In the Ute language of Colorado's first inhabitants,
sinapu means 'wolves'."*

Sinapu
P.O. Box 3243
Boulder, CO 80307
(303) 237-6280

⊷ PURPOSE ⊷

"...the increase and diffusion of knowledge among men."

⊷ ACTIVITIES ⊷

Operation of 15 galleries and museums;
research projects in the arts, history and science

⊷ GIFTS ⊷

Catalog: jewelry, toys, calendars, ornaments,
scarves, cross-stitch kits, sculptures, books, ties, shawls, lamps,
music boxes, ceramics, purses, games, bird feeders, rugs,
paperweights, pocket knives, model airplanes,
musical instruments, globes, art prints

*"The world's largest complex of museums,
art galleries and research facilities"*

Smithsonian Institution
Department 0006
Washington, DC 20073-0006
(800) 322-0344 ♦ (202) 357-1826

⊸ PURPOSE ⊶

Recognize the great human potential of each
individual and offer those in need a hand, not a handout

⊸ ACTIVITIES ⊶

Housing, alcohol counseling and referral,
education, water projects, emergency aid

⊸ GIFTS ⊶

Catalog: limited edition prints, turquoise
jewelry, ceramic Indian pottery, rugs, belts, beads,
toys, coloring books, hand-carved and
hand-painted Indian ceremonial dolls

"Buy beautiful works of art and help save the American Indian!"

Southwest Indian Foundation
P.O. Box 86
Gallup, NM 87302-0001
(505) 863-4037

⊸ PURPOSE ⊱
Provide a loving home in a family-style
setting for abused and/or neglected children

⊸ ACTIVITIES ⊱
Welcoming the children into cottages
headed by married couples; guide the young
people while they learn life skills

⊸ GIFTS ⊱
Greeting cards made by the
children from recycled card fronts

"A non-sectarian facility for children ages five to eighteen"

St. Jude's Ranch for Children
P.O. Box 60100
Boulder City, NV 89006-0100
(702) 293-3131

STUDENT ENVIRONMENTAL ACTION COALITION

⊸ PURPOSE ⊱
Build power among students involved
in environmental and social justice action

⊸ ACTIVITIES ⊱
National conferences, marches, newsletter,
internship program, information clearinghouses

⊸ GIFTS ⊱
T-shirts

"Energy independence"

Student Environmental Action Coalition
P.O. Box 1168
Chapel Hill, NC 27514
(919) 967-4600

THE TARLTON FOUNDATION

◄ PURPOSE ►

Aid in the preservation of the earth's waters
through conservation-focused marine education
and research programs

◄ ACTIVITIES ►

Sea Camp, WhaleBus (a classroom on wheels),
Adopt-a-Beach programs for students, Project
OCEAN (marine science in the classroom)

◄ GIFTS ►

Adopt-A-Whale: adoption certificate,
color photo, a written description of your whale,
fact sheet on the California gray whale, quarterly
updates, $50; $25 for schools and youth groups

"Help protect whales by supporting the Tarlton Foundation."

The Tarlton Foundation
50 Francisco Street #103
San Francisco, CA 94133
(415) 433-3163

TIMBER WOLF INFORMATION NETWORK

⊸ PURPOSE ⊱
Increase public awareness and acceptance
of the wolf in its natural habitat and its ecological
role in the environment

⊸ ACTIVITIES ⊱
Workshops, seminars, educational
curriculum development, wolf monitoring

⊸ GIFTS ⊱
Adopt-A-Wolf Pack: certificate, photo, wolf video,
newsletter, learning resource list, history of your pack,
semiannual reports, $75; T-shirts, sweatshirts

"Preserving the wolf through education"

Timber Wolf Information Network
Waupaca Field Station
E 110 Emmons Creek Road
Waupaca, WI 54981
(715) 258-7247

⊸ PURPOSE ⊷
Create just and fair trade between Native
producers and socially responsible consumers of the Americas

⊸ ACTIVITIES ⊷
Help producers study the marketplace,
develop products and find fair-paying markets

⊸ GIFTS ⊷
Catalog: clothing, quilts, jewelry, calendars, books,
purses, wallets, overnight bags, notecards, tablecloths, blankets

"Clothing that LOOKS, FEELS, and DOES GOOD!"

TRADE WIND
P.O. Box 380
156 Drakes Lane
Summertown, TN 38483
(800) 445-1991

TREEDOM

⊸ PURPOSE ⊱
Rebuild and create forests

⊸ ACTIVITIES ⊱
Plant and care for trees

⊸ GIFTS ⊱
Tree planting: personalized certificate
with the location of your tree, periodic updates, $18

"Give the world a breath of fresh air. Plant a tree."

Treedom
2269 Chestnut Street #603
San Francisco, CA 94123
(800) TREEDOM

⊸ PURPOSE ⊷

Help heal the environment by challenging citizens
of the Los Angeles area to participate in the planting,
care and appreciation of trees and the urban forest

⊸ ACTIVITIES ⊷

Neighborhood and mountain tree planting; Citizen
Forester training program; Environmental Leadership
program for kids; campus forestry products

⊸ GIFTS ⊷

Tree dedications in memory of or in honor of the
person you specify for a donation of $10 or more;
dedicate a grove for $50 or more

"A gift of life, a gift for the future"

TreePeople
12601 Mulholland Drive
Beverly Hills, CA 90210
(818) 753-4600

⊸ Purpose ⊶

Plant fruit trees worldwide to protect our
environment and provide a self-renewing source of
nutrition for people in need

⊸ Activities ⊶

Funding, management and know-how to
people in developing countries to plant and care for
food-bearing trees to fight world hunger

⊸ Gifts ⊶

Tree Adventure Kit with seeds, instructions, container
(10 fruit trees will also be planted around the world in the name
of the recipient who will also receive a certificate), $10; T-shirts

"Trees for Life....a growing solution!"

Trees for Life
1103 Jefferson
Wichita, KS 67203
(316) 263-7294

━ PURPOSE ━
Protect children around the world and
help them realize fuller, richer, healthier lives

━ ACTIVITIES ━
Health care, safe water supply,
sanitation, nutrition, education, training

━ GIFTS ━
Catalog: greeting cards, mugs, books,
games, puzzles, notecards, giftwrap, address
books, ornaments, calendars

"United Nations Children's Fund"

UNICEF
331 East 38th Street
New York, NY 10016
(800) 553-1200, catalog orders ♦ (212) 686-5522

➤ PURPOSE ➤
Help anyone who has had ostomy surgery
(or related surgeries) return to a normal living

➤ ACTIVITIES ➤
Hospital visitation,
education, advocacy, publications

➤ GIFTS ➤
Notecards

"Thirty years of caring"

United Ostomy Association
36 Executive Park, Suite 120
Irvine, CA 92714
(714) 660-8624 ♦ (800) 826-0826

⊣ PURPOSE ⊢

Enrich the lives of children, youth and adults
with disabilities through programs in the arts

⊣ ACTIVITIES ⊢

Performances, exhibitions and workshops of
drama, dance, music, literature and the visual arts

⊣ GIFTS ⊢

Calendars, posters, notecards,
international ornaments, prints, original art

*"Meeting special challenges
through the universal language of the arts"*

Very Special Arts
1331 F Street, NW
Washington, DC 20004
(800) 933-8721

VOLUNTEERS FOR PEACE

⊸ PURPOSE ⊱
World community
development and conflict resolution

⊸ ACTIVITIES ⊱
International Workcamps
(a short-term "peace corps") in 36 countries

⊸ GIFTS ⊱
T-shirts, International Workcamp Directory
(of summer volunteer opportunities in 36 countries)

"Feeling good about our future"

Volunteers for Peace
42 Tiffany Road
Belmont, VT 05730
(802) 259-2759

⊰ Purpose ⊱
Achieve sanctuary
status for the Pond

⊰ Activities ⊱
Legislative bill requesting the state to change
Walden from a swim/recreation park to a nature sanctuary

⊰ Gifts ⊱
Adopt Walden (a 10' x 10' parcel): framable
certificate which will eventually have memorabilia
value, starting at $10; T-shirts

*"Return Walden to the natural,
forested condition of the days of Thoreau."*

Walden Forever Wild
Box 275
Concord, MA 01742
(203) 429-2839

Whale Adoption Project

Purpose

Help support marine mammal protection and research

Activities

Operate a whale rescue and research vessel, protect whale and dolphin habitats, advocate marine mammal protection worldwide

Gifts

Adopt-A-Whale: adoption certificate, photo of your own whale, newsletter, calendar, congratulatory letter, decal, biographical sketch of your whale, First Mate card, $15; Catalog: T-shirts, sweatshirts, wind chimes, books, toys, posters, totes, mugs, watches, prints

"I love my humpback whale."

Whale Adoption Project
International Wildlife Coalition
634 North Falmouth Highway, Dept 91MD
P.O. Box 388
North Falmouth, MA 02556-0388
(508) 564-9980

WHITE HOUSE
HISTORICAL
ASSOCIATION

━ PURPOSE ━

Historical and educational to enhance understanding,
appreciation and enjoyment of the White House

━ ACTIVITIES ━

Publications, acquisition of historical
furnishings and works of art, official portraits of the
Presidents and First Ladies

━ GIFTS ━

Ornaments, notecards,
postcards, slide sets, books, prints

*"Supporting and acquiring historical furnishings and
works of art for the White House's permanent collection"*

White House Historical Association
740 Jackson Place, NW
Washington, DC 20503
(202) 737-8292

⊷ PURPOSE ⊶

Instruct the general public on the importance
of the study and sound deer management of our
nation's white-tailed deer

⊷ ACTIVITIES ⊶

Conservation scholarships, habitat
redevelopment programs, legislation

⊷ GIFTS ⊶

Books, polo shirts, suspenders,
hats, belt buckles, mugs, collector plates

"Dedicated to sound deer management"

Whitetails Unlimited
P.O. Box 422
Sturgeon Bay, WI 54235
(800) 274-5471

WILD CANID SURVIVAL AND RESEARCH CENTER

◄ Purpose ►
Captive breeding facility for
endangered red and Mexican wolves

◄ Activities ►
Wolf recovery in the
wild; wolf education

◄ Gifts ►
Adopt-A-Wolf: adoption certificate, a photo
representative of your pack, updates, newsletters,
$100 to adopt a pack for one year

"Adopt-A-Wolf"

Wild Canid Survival and Research Center
P.O. Box 760
Eureka, MO 63025
(314) 938-5900

THE WILDERNESS SOCIETY

⊸ PURPOSE ⊶

Preserve wilderness and wildlife; protect
America's prime forests, parks, rivers, deserts and
shorelands; foster an American land ethic

⊸ ACTIVITIES ⊶

Legislation, education, conservation

⊸ GIFTS ⊶

T-shirts, sweatshirts, caps, fanny packs, shirts,
pants, mugs, posters, coloring books, knives,
calendars, videos, books, totes

"Saving our Ancient Forests"

The Wilderness Society
900 Seventeenth Street, N.W.
Washington, DC 20006-2596
(202) 833-2300

➤ PURPOSE ➤
Solve global environmental problems
with an emphasis on individual action

➤ ACTIVITIES ➤
Education, research, publications,
grassroots outreach programs

➤ GIFTS ➤
Books, T-shirts, sweatshirts,
videos, audios, cookbook

*"We invite you to make a conscious choice for
a peaceful and environmentally sustainable future."*

The Windstar Foundation
2317 Snowmass Creek Road
Snowmass, CO 81654
(303) 927-4777

WORLD AWARENESS

⊷ PURPOSE ⊷
Promote world awareness through
activities, products and financial assistance

⊷ ACTIVITIES ⊷
Cultural awareness programs by performing
artists, quarterly publication (World Awareness News),
products promoting awareness of the world,
financing of needed projects such as construction
of wells in poor areas of the world

⊷ GIFTS ⊷
Board games, computer
games, books, cassettes, notecards

"Great games for global learning!"

World Awareness
890 Twin Towers
Ypsilanti. MI 48198-3882
(313) 481-8860

⊶ PURPOSE ⊷
Preserve all birds, especially
birds of prey and parrots

⊶ ACTIVITIES ⊷
Breeding and releasing endangered species;
treating and returning injured birds to the wild; education

⊶ GIFTS ⊷
Adopt-A-Bird: adoption certificate, photo,
newsletter, species information and a biography of your
bird, starting at $50; T-shirts, jackets, hats, polo shirts,
sweatshirts, mugs, posters, pins, pencils, totes

"Preserve habitat to preserve diversity."

World Bird Sanctuary
P.O. Box 270270
St. Louis, MO 63127
(314) 938-6193 ♦ (225) 4390

WORLD GAME INSTITUTE

⊰ PURPOSE ⊱
Research and education for developing
solutions to global and local problems

⊰ ACTIVITIES ⊱
Software development, workshops,
research laboratory, developer of The World Game

⊰ GIFTS ⊱
Games, books, software,
maps, hats, T-shirts, pins

"Create a world that works."

World Game Institute
University City Science Center
3508 Market Street
Philadelphia, PA 19104
(215) 387-0220

⊸ PURPOSE ⊷

Eliminate hunger, disease and
poverty in Asia, Africa and Latin America

⊸ ACTIVITIES ⊷

Food production, community-based health, family
planning, water and sanitation, environmental conservation,
small business, programs promoting self-reliance

⊸ GIFTS ⊷

Books, craft items from
Peru and Nepal, notecards

"Partnership is a powerful process."

World Neighbors
4127 NW 122 Street
Oklahoma City, OK 73120-8869
(405) 752-9700 ♦ (800) 242-6387

WORLD WILDLIFE FUND

⤙ PURPOSE ⤚
Wildlife conservation

⤙ ACTIVITIES ⤚
Protect tropical forests; create and defend national parks
and reserves; help people in developing countries improve their
lives without sacrificing their surroundings; train
park guards and equip anti-poaching teams

⤙ GIFTS ⤚
Catalog: clothing, notecards, greeting cards, sculptures,
giftwrap, calendars, totes, ornaments, umbrellas, scarves, puzzles,
rugs, glassware, mugs, pens, prints, jewelry, books, music
cassettes, toys, kitchen items, desk accessories, mobiles,
duffel bags, director's chairs, towels

"Saving life on Earth"

World Wildlife Fund
P.O. Box 224
Peru, Indiana 46970
(800) 833-1600

THE XERCES SOCIETY

⤙ PURPOSE ⤚
Conservation of invertebrates and preservation of
critical ecosystems worldwide (Invertebrates are creatures
without backbones--including butterflies, beetles,
ants, worms and myriad creatures of the sea.)

⤙ ACTIVITIES ⤚
Biodiversity research and training in Madagascar;
Pacific Northwest old-growth forest project; magazine

⤙ GIFTS ⤚
Books, coloring books, T-shirts,
sweatshirts, videos, greeting cards

"Preserving the little things that run the world"

The Xerces Society
10 SW Ash Street
Portland, OR 97204
(503) 222-2788

THE YOSEMITE ASSOCIATION

⊰ PURPOSE ⊱
Education; support of Yosemite National Park
through funding of National Park Service interpretive
and research programs

⊰ ACTIVITIES ⊱
Cooperating association; publication and sale of
books and tapes; outdoor seminar program; Park
visitor information; special programs

⊰ GIFTS ⊱
Books, maps, videos,
audios, mugs, puzzles, games

"Yosemite: A Gift of Creation"

The Yosemite Association
P.O. Box 230
El Portal, CA 95318
(209) 379-2648

ZERO POPULATION GROWTH

⊸ PURPOSE ⊶
Achieve a sustainable balance between
population, resources and the environment in the
United States and worldwide

⊸ ACTIVITIES ⊶
Education, citizen action efforts,
legislation, media campaigns, publications

⊸ GIFTS ⊶
T-shirts, sweatshirts, pins, posters, books

"ZPG...for Earth's sake"

Zero Population Growth
1400 16th Street NW, Suite 320
Washington, DC 20036
(202) 332-2200

ZOOLOGICAL SOCIETY OF MILWAUKEE COUNTY

⊸ PURPOSE ⊷

Support the Milwaukee County Zoo; education
on the importance of wildlife and the environment;
conserve the environment and endangered species

⊸ ACTIVITIES ⊷

Support the Zoo in animal exhibit construction, improvements
and animal acquisition; educational programs on wildlife conservation;
take part in conservation programs that benefit
Zoo animals and animals in the wild

⊸ GIFTS ⊷

Adopt An Animal: certificate of sponsorship, fact sheet,
recognition on an in-zoo donor board for a year, an invitation
to the annual Family Reunion Pinic, starting at $15

"Join the Wildest Family Around."

Zoological Society of Milwaukee County
10005 W. Bluemound Road
Milwaukee, WI 53226
(414) 258-2333

What Causes Would You Like To Support?

Animals: Farm and Domestic
Animals: Marine
Animals: Wildlife
Animals: Zoos
Arts
Children
Education
Environment
Health and Rehabilitation
Historical Preservation
Homelessness and Housing
Horticulture
Humanitarian Service
Hunger
Literacy
Museums
Native Americans
Peace
Science
Third World Peoples

ANIMALS-FARM & DOMESTIC

ANIMALS-MARINE

ANIMALS-MARINE (CONT.)

ANIMALS-WILDLIFE

ANIMALS-WILDLIFE (CONT.)

WORLD
WILDLIFE FUND
Jungle print duffel bag ✦ $58.50

ANIMALS-WILDLIFE (CONT.)

ANIMALS-ZOOS

ANIMALS-ZOOS (CONT.)

ARTS

CHILDREN

CHILDREN (CONT.)

Muscular Dystrophy Association ✦ *page 99*
The Pediatric Cancer Research Foundation ✦ *page 118*
Save the Children ✦ *page 132*
St. Jude's Ranch for Children ✦ *page 147*
UNICEF ✦ *page 155*
Very Special Arts ✦ *page 157*

EDUCATION

Astronomical Society of the Pacific ✦ *page 32*
Berea College Crafts ✦ *page 36*
National Geographic Society ✦ *page 102*
The Pierpont Morgan Library ✦ *page 120*
Smithsonian Institution ✦ *page 145*
World Awareness ✦ *page 166*
World Game Institute ✦ *page 168*

ENVIRONMENT

Action on Smoking and Health (ASH) ✦ *page 10*
American Forestry Association ✦ *page 19*
The American Horticultural Society ✦ *page 22*
American Oceans Campaign ✦ *page 26*
American Rivers ✦ *page 27*
Appalachian Trail Conference ✦ *page 30*

ENVIRONMENT (CONT.)

SIERRA CLUB
Swiss army
knife ◆ $30.00

ENVIRONMENT (CONT.)

ENVIRONMENT (CONT.)

HEALTH & REHABILITATION

```
. . . . . . . . . . . . . . . . . . . . . . .
```

SECTION TWO

```
. . . . . . . . . . . . . . . . . . . . . . .
```

HISTORICAL PRESERVATION

HOMELESSNESS & HOUSING

HORTICULTURE

HUMANITARIAN SERVICE

HUMANITARIAN SERVICE (CONT.)

HUNGER

LITERACY

MUSEUMS

NATIVE AMERICANS

PEACE

SCIENCE

SECTION TWO

THIRD WORLD PEOPLES

SECTION THREE

Gifts Available and Where To Get Them

Adopt-An-Acre Programs
Adopt-An-Animal Programs
Art & Art Objects
Books
Calendars
Clothing
Computer Software
Crafts
Desk Supplies & Accessories
Foods
Giftwrap
Holiday Items
Housewares
Jewelry
Luggage
Miscellaneous
Outdoor Items
Personal Care Products
Science Equipment
Stationery
Toys
Tree Plantings
Trees to Plant at Home
Videos

SECTION THREE

ADOPT-AN-ACRE PROGRAMS

Including land protection and purchase programs.

ADOPT-AN-ANIMAL PROGRAMS

Including animal sponsorship programs.

ADOPT-AN-ANIMAL PROGRAMS (CONT.)

ART & ART OBJECTS

Including bronzes, ceramic figurines, etchings, granite name engravings, original art, posters, prints, sculptures, statues, wood carvings.

ART & ART OBJECTS (CONT.)

CENTER FOR MARINE
CONSERVATION
Cast paper art, framed ◆ $45.00

ART & ART OBJECTS (CONT.)

SMITHSONIAN
Verdigris elephant
sculpture ✦ $45.00

ART & ART OBJECTS (CONT.)

BOOKS

Including bookmarks, cookbooks, diaries, and magazine subscriptions.

BOOKS (CONT.)

UNICEF
Two mugs,
set ✦ $18.00

BOOKS (CONT.)

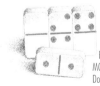

PIERPONT
MORGAN LIBRARY
Dominos ◆ $18.50

BOOKS (CONT.)

CALENDARS

CALENDARS (CONT.)

SHARE OUR
STRENGTH
Calendar ✦ $10.00

CLOTHING

Including aprons, bandanas, batiks, belts, caps, children's wear, hats, headbands, jackets, mohair stoles, neckties, nightshirts, pants, polo shirts, scarves, shawls, shirts, shoelaces, suspenders, sweatshirts/pants/jackets, T-shirts, visors, windbreakers.

CLOTHING (CONT.)

WHALE
ADOPTION
PROJECT
Dolphin tie
$10.95

CLOTHING (CONT.)

CHICAGO
FUND RAISING
COMMITTEE TO
BENEFIT PEDIATRIC
AIDS Shirts by Zack
$15.00

CLOTHING (CONT.)

PUEBLO TO PEOPLE Toddler rompers ◆ $17.00

CLOTHING (CONT.)

COMPUTER SOFTWARE

CRAFTS

Including cross stitch, handcrafts from around the world, stitchery kits.

CRAFTS (CONT.)

DESK SUPPLIES & ACCESSORIES

Including paperweights, pencils, pens.

FOODS

Including apples, caramel and chocolate covered apples, cheeses, chocolates, coffee, gourmet food baskets, gourmet sweet onions, pears, Rainforest Crunch.

FOODS (CONT.)

GIFTWRAP

HOLIDAY ITEMS

Including Christmas cards, greeting cards,
tree ornaments, wreaths.

```
. . . . . . . . . . . . . . . . . . . . . . .
```

SECTION THREE

```
. . . . . . . . . . . . . . . . . . . . . . .
```

HOLIDAY ITEMS (CONT.)

BETTER HOMES
FOUNDATION
Wreath ◆ $29.95

HOLIDAY ITEMS (CONT.)

HOUSEWARES

Including baskets, bedspreads, blankets, bookends, brooms, candles, candlesticks, chairs, china, coasters, crockery, cutting boards, dinnerware, enamelware, fireplace accessories, furniture, glassware, home decor, kitchen items, lamps, linens, mirrors, mugs, nesting boxes, pewter, porcelain tea sets, pottery, quilts, rugs, stemware, tablecloths, tableware, trays, trivets, towels.

HOUSEWARES (CONT.)

NATIONAL MUSEUM
OF WOMEN
IN THE ARTS
Peter Rabbit picture
frame ◆ $12.50

HOUSEWARES (CONT.)

JEWELRY

Including beads, belt buckles, bolo ties, pins, tie tacks, watches.

JEWELRY (CONT.)

SERRV
SELF-HELP
HANDCRAFTS
Hummingbird
pin ◆ $19.50

JEWELRY (CONT.)

LUGGAGE

Including duffel bags, fanny/hip packs, overnight bags, totes.

LUGGAGE (CONT.)

THE HUMANE SOCIETY OF THE UNITED STATES Tote ◆ $14.95

LUGGAGE (cont.)

MISCELLANEOUS

Collector plates, dog leashes, family trees, gift bags, gift baskets, gifts related to nature and plants, key chains/tags/rings, lunch bags, mobiles, music boxes, purses, rafting trips, rain forest products, umbrellas, wallets.

MISCELLANEOUS (CONT.)

MUSICAL INSTRUMENTS

OUTDOOR ITEMS

Including backpacks, bat detectors, bat houses, bird feeders, flashlights, gardening supplies, garden ornaments, lanterns, naturalist's tools, pocket knives, sports water bottles, suncatchers, Swiss army knives, walking sticks, wind-bells, wind chimes, windsocks.

OUTDOOR ITEMS (CONT.)

PERSONAL CARE PRODUCTS

Including body care products and rainforest soaps.

SCIENCE EQUIPMENT

Globes, maps, observing aids.

STATIONERY

Including address books, all-occasion cards, greeting cards, notecards, notepads, postcards.

ASPCA
Notecards
$10.00

STATIONERY (CONT.)

SAVE THE
CHILDREN Christmas
cards ✦ $10.95

STATIONERY (CONT.)

TOYS

Including banks, board games, coloring books, computer games, dolls, educational games, model airplanes, puppets, puzzles, rubber stamps, stuffed toys.

TOYS (CONT.)

ART INSTITUTE OF CHICAGO
Madeline book and doll ◆ $48.95

TOYS (CONT.)

TREE PLANTINGS

TREES TO PLANT AT HOME

Including seeds and Tree Adventure Kits.

VIDEOS & AUDIOS

Including CD's, music, slides, soundtracks.

NATIONAL
WILDLIFE
FEDERATION
John Denver's
Earth Songs
CD ✦ $14.95

VIDEOS & AUDIOS (CONT.)

OXFAM AMERICA Hand-carved wooden animals set ◆ $19.95

BIBLIOGRAPHY

Buzzworm Magazine. *1992 Earth Journal: Environmental Almanac and Resources Directory*. Boulder, Colorado: Buzzworm Books, 1992.

Carroll, Andrew. *Volunteer USA*. New York: Fawcett Columbine, 1991.

Earthworks Group, The. *50 Simple Things You Can Do To Save The Earth*. Berkeley, California: Earthworks Press, 1989.

Earthworks Group, The. *The Next Step: 50 More Things You Can Do To Save The Earth*. Kansas City: Andrews and McMeel, 1991.

Fox, Dr. Michael W., Pamela Weintraub. *You Can Save the Animals: 50 Things To Do Right Now*. New York: St. Martin's Press, 1991.

Gershen, Howard. *A Guide for Giving: 250 Charities and How They Use Your Money*. New York: Pantheon Books, 1990.

Hollender, Jeffrey. *How To Make The World A Better Place: A Guide to Doing Good*. New York: William Morrow & Co., 1990.

Lanier-Graham, Susan D. *The Nature Directory: A Guide to Environmental Organizations*. New York: Walker and Co., 1991.

Lawson, Douglas M. *Give to Live: How Giving Can Change Your Life*. La Jolla, California: ALTI Publishing, 1991.

BIBLIOGRAPHY

Levine, Michael. *The Environmental Address Book: How to Reach the Environment's Greatest Champions and Worst Offenders.* New York: Perigee Books, 1991.

Lewis, Scott. *The Rainforest Book: How You Can Save the World's Rainforests.* Los Angeles: Living Planet Press, 1990.

Living Planet Press. *The Animal Rights Handbook: Everyday Ways To Save Animal Lives.* Los Angeles: Living Planet Press, 1990.

Luks, Allen. *The Healing Power of Doing Good: The Health and Spiritual Benefits of Helping Others.* New York: Fawcett Columbine, 1991.

Lynberg, Michael. *The Gift of Giving.* New York: Fawcett Columbine, 1991.

Mackey, Philip English. *The Giver's Guide: Making Your Charity Dollars Count.* Highland Park, New Jersey: Catbird Press, 1990

Makower, Joel, ed. *The Nature Catalog.* New York: Vintage Books, 1991.

Newkirk, Ingrid. *Save the Animals!: 101 Easy Things You Can Do.* New York: Warner Books, 1990

Rifkin, Jeremy, ed. *The Green Lifestyle Handbook.* New York: Henry Holt & Company, 1990

BIBLIOGRAPHY

Salzman, Marian, Teresa Reisgies, *150 Ways Teens Can Make A Difference*. Princeton, New Jersey: Petersen's Guides, 1991

Sequoia, Anna. *67 Ways to Save the Animals*. New York: Harper Collins Publishers, 1990.

Seredich, John, ed. *Your Resource Guide to Environmental Organizations*. Irvine, California: Smiling Dolphins Press, 1991.

Sorg, Leslie, *Gifting Right*. Los Angeles: CCC Publications, 1990

Tuckerman, Nancy. *In the Tiffany Style: Gift-Giving for All Occasions*. New York: Doubleday, 1990

Vallely, Bernadette. *1,001 Ways to Save the Planet*. New York: Ivy Books, 1990

World Resources Institute, comp. *The 1992 Information Please Environmental Almanac*. Boston: Houghton Mifflin Company, 1992.

Zimmerman, Richard. *What Can I Do To Make A Difference?: A Positive Action Sourcebook*. New York: Penguin Books 1991.

NATIONAL PARKS &
CONSERVATION ASSOCIATION
Stuffed bear • $15.95

NATIONAL ARCHIVES
TRUST FUND
Smokey bear
$25.00

AMERICAN
DIABETES
ASSOCIATION
Teddy bear
$10.00

SMITHSONIAN
Teddy bear
$22.00

AMERICAN LIBRARY
ASSOCIATION
Paddington bear
$12.00

Z

If you would like your organization to be included in another book in this series or if corrections should be made to current text for an updated edition of *GIFTS THAT MAKE A DIFFERENCE*, please send the appropriate information to:

Foxglove Publishing
P.O. Box 292500
Dayton, Ohio 45429-0500
USA

▲

To order a copy of *GIFTS THAT MAKE A DIFFERENCE*, please send $7.95 plus $2.00, handling and shipping, to:

Foxglove Publishing
P.O. Box 292500
Dayton, Ohio 45429-0500
USA